If there was ever a day when God  to invite His manifest presence every direction we look in our cu God is dismissed from a culture, it is incumbent upon God's people, through whom He has determined to express His presence, to make contact with Him, in unity, in one accord. So: I'd encourage you and your church to get involved, read this book, and make your voices heard on earth, inviting heaven into our midst, to turn around a culture in chaos.

DR. TONY EVANS
founder and president of The Urban Alternative

John Bornschein's new book brings to light the true power that is in the hands of the followers of Jesus Christ when those hands are clasped in earnest, interceding prayer. *A Prayer Warrior's Guide to Spiritual Battle* will help you better understand both why and how you can prevail in prayer over your family and even this nation. I am confident that this great book by a true national prayer leader will kindle prayer fires in you that God can use to deliver men and nations!

TONY PERKINS
president of Family Research Council

I am truly excited about *A Prayer Warrior's Guide to Spiritual Battle!* This book is a gift to believers everywhere who want to draw closer to the Lord and be part of His activity through prayer. Drawn from the wealth of knowledge shared by trusted spiritual leaders and members of the National Prayer Committee—many of whom I consider dear friends—this comprehensive *Prayer Warrior's Guide* will open your heart and mind to experience the fullness of the power of prayer through relationship with Christ. This *Guide* dives deep in content but remains accessible and practical. From new believers to seasoned spiritual leaders, everyone will find fresh wisdom and direction for an effective, meaningful, and life-giving prayer life.

DR. DICK EASTMAN
international president of Every Home for Christ

A Prayer Warrior's Guide to Spiritual Battle is a great resource for those who want to better understand how to effectively engage in spiritual warfare on the front lines in our culture. The insights and practical truths on prayer will encourage all.

DAVID KUBAL
president of Intercessors for America

Faith has always been the golden strand that binds Americans together—faith not only in the promises and benefits of freedom, but ultimately, in the grace and benevolence of the Creator whose hand has sustained and upheld this country throughout its history. Our world is in desperate need of people of prayer—individuals who will cry out to God day and night for transformation of the hearts and minds of all men. *A Prayer Warrior's Guide to Spiritual Battle* is the kindling for a spiritual fire of the soul to go deeper with God in solemn assembly.

DAVID BARTON
founder and president of WallBuilders

I cannot think of a more significant focus than the one this book addresses. We are in the greatest spiritual battle of our lifetimes. What a blessing to have these seasoned prayer leaders offer their insights as to how we can be prayer warriors used of God to help win the battle!

PAUL CEDAR
chairman, Mission America Coalition

A PRAYER WARRIOR'S GUIDE TO SPIRITUAL BATTLE

Also by John Bornschein
published by Kirkdale Press

For Life: Defending the Defenseless

A PRAYER WARRIOR'S GUIDE TO SPIRITUAL BATTLE

The Front Line

JOHN BORNSCHEIN

EDITOR

with
Ashley Bornschein, David Butts, Kathy Branzell,
Dion Elmore, Linda Rutzen, Kara Schwab,
Brian Toon, and Robert Velarde

KIRKDALE PRESS

A Prayer Warrior's Guide to Spiritual Battle: The Front Line
2nd Edition

Copyright 2016 John Bornschein

Kirkdale Press, 1313 Commercial St., Bellingham, WA 98225
Visit us at KirkdalePress.com or follow us on Twitter at @KirkdalePress

Print ISBN 9781577996897
Digital ISBN 9781577996972

Kirkdale Editorial: Elizabeth Vince, Abigail Stocker
Cover Design: Patrick Fore
Back Cover Design: Brittany Schrock
Typesetting: ProjectLuz.com

After they prayed, the place where they were meeting was shaken. And they were all filled with the Holy Spirit and spoke the word of God boldly.

—Acts 4:31

CONTENTS

FOREWORD

On a small ranch in Wyoming a man went out to protect his cattle from an approaching tornado as his wife and child looked on. With a sudden turn, the tornado moved directly toward him. His wife excitedly turned to their son and said, "Johnny, quick! Get on your knees and pray!" Johnny instantly fell to his knees and began to say: "Now I lay me down to sleep..." It was the only thing he had ever said to God! This fictitious story should remind us of the importance of teaching our children to pray. Without proper understanding, they cannot pray effectively. Many of them learn to recite a model, but don't comprehend how to communicate with Jesus Christ. We need to help them realize that God desires a relationship with them—and it is not just our children who need to understand the power of prayer. The foundation of nations is built on prayer; therefore, we as adults need to learn how to pray. America is in need of revival as perhaps never before, and only in prayer will we find restoration and revelation.

Relationship is the core of effective prayer. Each of us has been given the ability to come before God's throne of grace (Heb 4:16) at any time to communicate with our Creator. This is one of the truths that makes our faith unique, but it can be difficult for our minds to grasp. On an earthly level, we are not accustomed to this kind of unlimited access to those in authority, but

God is different. We can approach Him in an instant. He wants to hear from us and is pleased when we call! He will never put us "on hold," tell us He will respond later, take His "phone" off the hook, or let an answering machine take our message.

Jesus Christ wants a relationship with us that is built on time spent in His presence and reading His Word. On a personal level, we can speak to Him about anything and everything. And yet, although prayer is simple, its principles must be learned. Even the disciples asked their Master to teach them to pray.

There is no underestimating the importance of prayer in a family or its influence and vital importance in our nation. I feel this very strongly because it was so decidedly absent from my own early childhood experience. The little girl that I once was grew up in a troubled home where daily prayers were unknown and the sounds of joyful praise were never heard. I'm aware of what family-centered spiritual training can mean to a child because I "discovered" it for myself when I was about eight years old. What a contrast to the rich spiritual heritage of my husband's family! He has often told me how his grandmother used to gather the six children around her for daily devotions. She prayed, "Lord, it is my most urgent request that each of these children will come to know You personally. If one of them fails to make that commitment, it would have been better that I never had been born." This is the priority she gave to her spiritual responsibility. Her prayers made such an impression on Jim's dad that he referred to them throughout his life. This is the example our children need to see in us. But it is more than a model. Prayer and reverence for God must permeate every aspect of our lives and become a natural part of our lives.

We need to learn how to become a people of prayer once again. Then—and only then—will God hear us from heaven and restore and heal our land.

Shirley Dobson
Chairman, National Day of Prayer Task Force

INTRODUCTION

At this point, you have probably picked up a book or two on prayer. Perhaps dialogue with the Almighty is something that you are seeking to learn more about, and deep down you know you've only scratched the surface. Well, you have taken a bold step. This book will both challenge and empower you, and through the journey, you will gain a greater understanding of the weapons of our warfare on the spiritual battlefield.

The front line is the threshold where the battle is won or lost. It is the turning point for victory or defeat, where the will of the mind prevails over flesh through faith and the empowering of the Holy Spirit. Just as Gideon and his 300 warriors stood firm in the face of the enemy, we must be bold for truth in a society of moral relativism. Courage under fire requires a necessary balance of prayer and Scripture study within the church body—harmony between order and discipline. It is the fortitude of knowledge and unity to bring down barriers and move mountains in our culture.

Preparation for battle requires advanced training for men and women of faith. Scripture tells us that "Anyone who lives on milk, being still an infant, is not acquainted with the teaching about righteousness. But solid food is for the mature, who by constant use have trained themselves to distinguish good from evil" (Heb 5:13-14). The battlefield is real, and the devil is very aware of you. In fact, he is a roaring lion looking for someone to devour (1 Pet 5:8), and he has you in his sights. Why? Because if you are a Christian, you are a child of the living God. You have power that the human mind cannot fully comprehend, and this power is unleashed through prayer. The adversary knows your potential, and he will stop at nothing to prevent you from accomplishing your mission here on earth. He will strike at every area of your life to bring you down. But "count it all joy" (Jas 1:2 NKJV), for once you know what the devil knows about who you are in Christ Jesus, you will stand boldly at the front lines, seeing only victory, not defeat.

PRAYER IS THE WORK

Someone once said that we make a mistake when we think of praying for God's work to be done. "We don't pray *for* the work," he said, "prayer *is* the work." You have a lot of tasks ahead of you, but they all pale in importance compared to the priority of prayer. Remember John 15—we're the branches on the vine. Branches don't work and strive to produce fruit; that happens naturally as a result of their connection to the vine. Don't let your "to-do" lists—as important as they are—sever your connection with the Vine. Work in a context of prayer. Plan in a context of prayer. Make your contacts in a context of prayer.

The authors who contributed to this resource have spent decades studying prayer in depth and have compiled this book as a field manual to prepare you for spiritual warfare. The battlefield is multidimensional and must be fought on several fronts. There are times to get your hands dirty and there are times to get your knees dirty. On your knees, you will wage a war that is not bound by the borders of the sea, air, or land. These battles must be fought simultaneously, for physical strongholds are spiritually sustained one way or another. In the art of war, you do not strike the enemy from one side alone; you must employ a multifaceted strategy, attacking the enemy from all sides.

The dominion of darkness is at work all over our planet with the sole purpose of destroying humankind and taking the birthright that is freely given to those who accept the gift to be heirs of the Most High. The armies of our adversary know who the soldiers of the kingdom are, and they know those who are not (Acts 19:13–16). They are also afraid and know their time is short (Jas 2:18–19; Rev 12:12).

Right now, you may be willing to jump into the fight and build a lasting legacy that will never erode and has eternal blessing. That is honorable. However, before you can walk in the Valley of Elah and take on Goliath, you must be trained in the discipline of spiritual warfare. To be a true prayer warrior is the highest, most effective level a combatant in the kingdom can attain. Everything done under the heavens is accomplished through prayer. Nothing will stand against the forces of evil without it.

An incredible connection is formed between believers and the heavenly Father during prayer. This connection is something that intersects the physical with the spiritual and goes far beyond human comprehension. The ability for humankind to speak in the throne room of the Almighty is awesome in and of itself. But the fact that God in all of His splendor will stop and listen intently to our every word, as if nothing could be more important to Him at that moment, is truly breathtaking. God desires relationship with us, and our dialogue with Him through prayer is where He reveals the deepest characteristics of His nature. In the book of Philippians, the apostle Paul reminds us that our determined purpose is to become more deeply and intimately acquainted with God. There is great power in this fellowship.

You have been called for such a time as this to be a light in a dark world. I challenge you now to continue your training and learn what real hand-to-hand combat is all about.

"Now to Him who is able to do exceedingly abundantly above all that we ask or think, according to the power that works in us, to Him *be* glory in the church by Christ Jesus to all generations, forever and ever. Amen."

(Ephesians 3:20-21 NKJV)

NATIONAL PRAYER

BILLY GRAHAM

Our Father and our God,

We praise You for Your goodness to our nation, giving us blessings far beyond what we deserve.

Yet we know all is not right with America. We deeply need a moral and spiritual renewal to help us meet the many problems we face.

Convict us of sin. Help us to turn to You in repentance and faith. Set our feet on the path of Your righteousness and peace.

We pray today for our nation's leaders. Give them the wisdom to know what is right, and the courage to do it.

You have said, "Blessed is the nation whose God is the LORD."[1] May this be a new era for America, as we humble ourselves and acknowledge You alone as our Savior and Lord.

This we pray in Your holy name,

Amen.[2]

CHAPTER 1

CALL TO WAR

JOHN BORNSCHEIN

In the powerful work *Giving Ourselves to Prayer*, Gary T. Meadors observes that dialogue with the Almighty is part of the fabric of the Bible: "Genesis 4:26 first mentions that 'men began to call on the name of the Lord,' and Revelation 22:20 closes the Bible with the prayer, 'Come, Lord Jesus' (compare 1 Cor 16:22). The entire history of redemption is framed in prayer. In between these terminal references we find a database about prayer that is so large it requires description beyond simple definition."[1] Why do we pray? Here are a few key reasons:[2]

1. **We love Him.** Just as a man and woman in love desire to be together and communicate, so we, if we love God, will desire to be with Him and to fellowship with Him in proportion to our love for Him.

2. **We depend on God.** He is our source. He is our life (Col 3:4). Through prayer, we receive the comfort, strength, and all the other resources we need in life, both naturally and spiritually. Prayer—relationship with God—is as necessary to the spiritual life as air is to the natural life.

3. **Prayer allows us to resist temptation**. Jesus warned His disciples to "watch and pray, lest you enter into

temptation" (Matt 26:41 NKJV). Living a life without prayer can leave us weak and exposed, giving an opportunity for the enemy to gain ground and potentially lure us into sin.

4. **Prayer is necessary for people to invite God to act in salvation.** God gave the earth to Adam and his descendants, so we must invite God to work here. If no one invites Him to work on earth, Satan—the "god of this age" because of humanity's universal rebellion (2 Cor 4:4)—will dominate human affairs, and eventually the judgment of God will come. By inviting God to intercede often and specifically, multitudes can be saved who would otherwise be lost.

5. **God commands us to pray.** In Colossians 4:2, Paul writes: "Continue earnestly in prayer, being vigilant in it with thanksgiving" (NKJV). Jesus also encouraged His followers to pray: "Then He [Jesus] spoke a parable to them, that men always ought to pray and not lose heart" (Luke 18:1 NKJV).

The need to pray is as great as the authority of God, who commands us to "pray without ceasing" (1 Thess 5:17 NKJV). Prayer is so vital to all that God wants to do on the earth, and it is so essential to us, that He commands us to do it all the time. We should even deny ourselves sleep and food at times to pray more and with greater power (see Matt 6:16; Luke 6:12; 21:36; Col 4:2; 2 Cor 11:27). Or, as John Chrysostom wrote:

> Prayer has subdued the strength of fire. It has bridled the rage of lions, hushed anarchy to rest, extinguished wars, appeased the elements, burst the chains of death, expanded the fates of heaven, assuaged diseases, dispelled frauds, rescued cities from destruction, staid the sun in its course, and arrested the progress of the thunderbolt. In this communion with God, there is an all-sufficient panoply, a treasure undiminished,

a mine that is never exhausted, a sky unobscured by
clouds, a heaven unruffled by the storm. It is the root,
the fountain, the mother of a thousand blessings![3]

Using information gleaned from a 2008 poll about spirituality
in America, *Parade Magazine* noted: "Our nation was built on
a foundation of strong faith, and in some respects, that hasn't
changed." The poll found that "69% of Americans believe in
God, 77% pray outside of religious services, and 75% believe it's a
parent's responsibility to give children a religious upbringing."
In contrast to speculation that "a new atheism" is at rise in the
United States, this study found that "only 5% of respondents
didn't believe in God. ... [In fact,] 67% said they pray because it
brings them comfort and hope."[4]

The National Day of Prayer Task Force, where I serve as
vice chairman, began calling the nation to prayer in 1991 under
the leadership of Mrs. Shirley Dobson. As millions gathered
each year in solemn assembly asking the Lord to intervene in
America, He answered in numerous ways. We can't directly tie
declines in negative cultural statistics to prayer, but the timing
is certainly worth taking note of. Between 1994 and 2008, the
violent crime rate in America decreased 17.7 percent, and the
property crime rate decreased 19.5 percent.[5]

The role of prayer in America cannot be ignored. Jennifer
Harper of the *Washington Times* writes, "Politicians come and go,
fashions evolve and the culture shifts with alarming frequen-
cy. One thing remains constant, though. Americans pray. A lot.
Ninety percent have a spiritual interlude with God every day,
according to a study released Thursday by Brandeis University.
Half pray several times a day, in fact."[6]

The National Day of Prayer website has cited numerous stories of answered prayers that have made headline news across
the country, including the following report published by the
task force in 2009:[7]

In big cities and small towns, Christians are using their faith and prayers to combat crime, homelessness, corruption and economic doldrums.

Following a forty-day prayer vigil organized by the Orlando Police Department, a dramatic decrease in crime was reported. The goal was to reduce crime in Orlando by taking God's word outside of churches and onto the streets. "We want to come to the street and bring the love and the compassion of our lord, Jesus Christ, to the community," said Angel Torres, an Orlando Police Department chaplain.

The report goes on to detail similar cases of answered prayers in communities, including Washington, D.C.; Manchester, Kentucky; and "dozens of towns, from Georgia to Texas." Through the tireless efforts of citizens submitting petitions, as well as the diligent work of the Alliance Defending Freedom, the Family Research Council, and WallBuilders, concerted efforts to strip away the faith of this nation have been repeatedly thwarted. But the opponents of faith won't stay silent. Even so, the National Day of Prayer has persevered despite several lawsuits from non-Christian organizations.

The voice of the saints cannot be ignored.

Without prayer, none of these victories would have been won. Before Proposition 8 went to a vote in California, tens of thousands filled Qualcomm Stadium in San Diego to fast and pray in support of traditional marriage.[8] And when the National Day of Prayer became the subject of a federal lawsuit, more than 250,000 people joined together to support the day via social media.[9] Millions of people gathered across the world on the Global Day of Prayer, and more than one million believers marched through the streets of Mexico City, shouting praises to the Lord while they fasted and prayed. Across the country, 24-hour houses of prayer began springing up. In 2015, the National Day of Prayer saw more than 43,000 prayer gatherings happen— the most gatherings in the National Day of Prayer's history.[10]

The victories belong to God, but the body of Christ knew they had to act in faith, lifting each matter before Him and seeking His intervention. The Prayer Movement is alive and well, gaining momentum as never before.

DOES PRAYER WORK?

Prayer is making a difference, transforming the landscape of homes and communities across the globe. A Lifeway Research survey estimates that 70 percent of Christian teens and young adults will walk away from the church during college. In the survey, participants who didn't leave the church (at all or permanently) indicated that parents who were examples of commitment to the church made a difference in influencing their children's decisions to stay.[11] You may have heard the saying, "A couple that prays together, stays together." Although we know this to be true, it is helpful to examine the evidence that best supports this common perception. An article published in the *Journal of Social and Clinical Psychology* had this to say about prayer:[12] "There is some evidence that religiosity is similarly related to several positive relationship outcomes. Specifically, greater involvement in religious activities [including prayer] is related to higher levels of marital satisfaction ... and marital stability with three longitudinal studies indicating that religiousness predicts lower risk of divorce and divorce proneness." The report goes on to cite that "prayer may help couples to more often 'think of the needs of others, be more loving and forgiving, treat each other with respect, and resolve conflict.' "[13] The researchers suggest that the relationship people experience with God through prayer helps them handle their emotions, be more empathetic, become less self-focused, and gain greater skills in reconciliation. They also note that "prayer for the partner might prime partners to think about each other in more loving or compassionate terms and so treat each other with greater respect and sensitivity."

Praying regularly together also "helped couples prevent conflict in their relationships." Researchers note that couples who included "God in their marriage through prayer" were more skilled in problem solving and reconciliation. Other couples "reported that prayer alleviated tension and facilitated open communication during conflict."

BEYOND THE HOME

Even if God didn't answer the prayers of His people, the positive effects of prayer are undeniable. When a father prays for his children, what is he demonstrating in that action? He is showing them true humility, compassion, and love. He is also showing that he is accountable to someone bigger than himself and that there is a structured chain of command that keeps the family healthy and aligned.

With this in mind, imagine what the action of prayer does for a community. If religious leaders are praying for civil leaders, they are honoring that which God has put in place. As Romans 13:1 states, "Let everyone be subject to the governing authorities, for there is no authority except that which God has established." Paul also encouraged believers to pray for their leaders: "I urge ... that petitions, prayers, intercession and thanksgiving be made for all people—for kings and all those in authority, that we may live peaceful and quiet lives in all godliness and holiness. This is good, and pleases God our Savior, who wants all people to be saved and to come to a knowledge of the truth" (1 Tim 2:1-4).

A nation can be punished by the actions of its leaders (2 Sam 24), and a nation can be punished with poor leaders because the hearts of the people are evil (2 Kgs 17:1-23; Isa 1; Jer 3). In the same way, a nation can be blessed with good leadership because the people honor God (Prov 8:14-16; 2 Chr 7:14). We can honor the structure of leadership that God has ordained (Exod 18:21; Deut 17:14-20), and we can do this even if we do not agree with all the decisions those in authority are making; that's all the more reason to pray for them.

2002
NATIONAL PRAYER
LLOYD OGILVIE

Gracious God,

All that we have and are is a result of Your amazing generosity. Since September 11, in the battle against terrorism we have discovered again that You truly are our refuge and strength, an ever-present help in trouble.

We rededicate ourselves to be one nation under You. In You we trust. We reaffirm our accountability to You, to the absolutes of Your Commandments, and to justice in our society.

Bless our president, Congress, and all our leaders with supernatural power. We commit ourselves to be faithful to You as sovereign of our land and as our personal Lord and Savior.

Amen.

CHAPTER 2

THE BASELINE

JOHN BORNSCHEIN

The action of prayer is healthy for a home and a community. We know that God does hear these prayers, which is where the real power resides. You would not be reading this book unless you had some inkling that there is a Creator who you are accountable to and are seeking to understand more about His nature and how to dialogue with Him. This is the baseline that you must recognize before you make any further efforts to unravel the mysteries of prayer.

There is no basis for understanding prayer without first proclaiming that without a doubt, there is a God in heaven who created you and desires fellowship with you. As Anthony DeStefano states so well in his book, *Ten Prayers God Always Says Yes To*:

> There isn't much room for compromise here. Either we're alone in the world or we're not. Either we came about by chance or we were created for a reason. Either death is the end or it's the beginning. Either our situation is ultimately hopeless or it's ultimately blissful. There really can't be two more different or diametrically opposed worldviews. So how can we come to grips with this most profound question? Some

of the greatest geniuses the world has ever known—
Aristotle, Plato, Augustine, Aquinas, Spinoza, Pascal,
Descartes and Kant, to name a few—have made the
case that there is a God, and that He is a real, living
being. In the case of faith, it's easy to overlook the most
fundamental point of all, namely, that God is not an ar-
gument; he is not a syllogism; he is not even a concept.
God is a living being. He has the ability to know things,
to desire things, to create things, and to love things. He
is fully aware and involved. He is alive.[1]

Theology is our understanding of God. The term literally means
"*logos* about *Theos*," or a "word about God." The Christian faith
is built on the foundation of trust in Almighty God who has
revealed Himself to humanity. God the Father is the one who
created the universe and sustains it, all while desiring a relationship with each one of us. "Almighty" means that God is sovereign over His creation. With wisdom and love, and in power
and control, God presides over all things. His sovereignty is a
source of comfort and truth for believers; we know that nothing
happens without His knowledge and permission.

The words "Creator of heaven and earth" reflect our belief
that all things were created by an orderly, wise God. Life has
meaning and purpose. Humans bear God's image and likeness;
therefore, all of life is to be respected, and creation should be
valued. The complexity and design of the world around us
lead us to the conclusion that there must be a grand designer
or Creator. Empirical evidence found in life, chemistry, astro-
biology, and especially physics suggests purpose, design, order,
and meaning. Psalm 19:1 tells us that the created world points to
the God who was its infinite originating source: "The heavens
declare (or "bear witness to") the glory of God; the skies (or "expanse") proclaim the work of his hands."

What separates God from the rest of the spiritual or unseen entities, or even that which is in the physical world, is the
fact that He is the *only* source of creation and life. There is no

tangible evidence that suggests otherwise. God, Yahweh, the Alpha and the Omega, the only God by many names created the vast expanse of the universe and all that is within it, along with all dimensions, space, and time and the beings that inhabit them. And He created all of this from absolutely nothing. In fact, the human body is one of the most complex machines ever created. The bacterial flagellum is only between one and two microns in size, and yet it is one of most efficient rotary motors on the planet.

One cannot look at the universe and not see intelligent design. Human beings have created nothing. We have manipulated and shaped elements and worked within the confines of natural laws, but we have never created something from nothing. Even the theory of evolution is based on the "change in the inherited traits of a population of organisms from one generation to the next." It is the theory of natural selection over a large span of time. Regardless of the amount of time that is required for evolution to take place, the theory self-destructs when origin is examined. There is no beginning to the process that has a viable source without a Creator. Thus, we are right back to confronting the fact that an intelligent designer is at work, an engineer of a very complex system. R. C. Sproul writes that "men are never duly touched and impressed with a conviction of their insignificance, until they have contrasted themselves with the majesty of God."[2]

IMAGE OF GOD

If indeed there is a God, are we created in His likeness? The answer to this question is critical for establishing a baseline when discussing the principles of prayer and the origin of its power. According to Dr. Michael Behe, biophysics professor at Lehigh University, one could argue that the human body is more complex than the earth and its entire ecological system. However, is this vessel and its complexity what God was referring to when

He stated in Genesis 1:26, "Let us make mankind in our image, in our likeness"?

Genesis 1:27 observes, "So God created mankind in his own image, in the image of God he created them; male and female he created them." Is the image of God the vessel of the human body, or is it something more? This is where we must begin in order to unravel the interpretation of this passage. Many scholars and theologians have attempted to answer the question, "What is the image of God?"

- Thomas Aquinas identified the image of God as "the human ability to think and reason, to use language and art, far surpassing the abilities of any animals."[3]

- Leonard Verduin stated that the image of God "consists in our dominion over animals and plants, which continues despite our sinfulness."[4]

- G. W. Bromiley notes, "A 'widely accepted interpretation' is that the 'image' is our ability to make moral decisions, which involve self-awareness and social awareness."[5]

- According to Emil Brunner, the image is "our ability to have a relationship with God, reflected in the tendency of all societies to have forms of worship."[6]

Many theologians believe there are three common elements within the concept of *imago Dei* (the "image of God"):

1. **Substantive:** The *substantive* element refers to the idea that humans were formed in the likeness of God in both characteristics and physical form. Many believe that God crafted our very design from His own makeup. According to this theory, God inhabits a body, and He used this perfect, flawless vessel as a blueprint for the human structure. In addition, we are formed in His likeness by our characteristics—our free will. We are not programmed by instinct, design, or function. We can execute decisions based on our thoughts. Martin Luther suggested that

humanity possessed the character of holiness—morality and love for God.

2. **Relational:** The *relational* element is based on the theology that we had a relationship with God before the fall of humanity, and to retain the image of God, we must have the Holy Spirit dwelling within us through a relationship with Christ. It is this gift that separates us from other complex living creatures. We are not organic machines. Rather, we are living souls that have a destination in the spiritual realm. We are symbiotic creations, evidenced by the fact that our living, breathing, physical body is controlled by a living soul.

3. **Functional:** The *functional* element focuses more on the second part of Genesis 1:26, which states, "They may rule over the fish in the sea and the birds in the sky, over the livestock and all the wild animals, and over all the creatures that move along the ground." This theory suggests that the authority over creation is the image of God. God has authority over all creation, but He has granted this authority to humankind over the earth. Thus, all creation on earth is subject to the rule of humankind, just as the universe is subject to God.

Now we must examine God's Word to pull the pieces together in our understanding of the image of God. Consider Psalm 139:14–16: "I praise you because I am fearfully and wonderfully made; your works are wonderful, I know that full well. My frame was not hidden from you when I was made in the secret place, when I was woven together in the depths of the earth. Your eyes saw my unformed body; all the days ordained for me were written in your book before one of them came to be." God tells the prophet Jeremiah something similar in Jeremiah 1:5—"Before I formed you in the womb I knew you, before you were born I set you apart." In both of these verses, we see a common thread: God knew the person before He made the body.

In the book of James, one of my favorite writings, we read two passages that build on this theme. James 3:9 states, "With the tongue we praise our Lord and Father, and with it we curse human beings, *who have been made in God's likeness*" (emphasis added). Later, James writes, "What is your life? *You are a mist that appears for a little while and then vanishes*" (Jas 4:14, emphasis added).

Do these verses contradict each other? If we are made in God's likeness, why does He use such blunt and even harsh words to describe the frailty of humanity? In chapter three, James is reprimanding us for "cursing" those who have been formed in God's likeness; yet only a few verses later, in chapter four, he tells us that we are nothing more than a mist—here today, gone tomorrow. Already, there is a distinction between the body and the soul.

Three verses from Genesis also stress that the body is limited—nothing more than flesh and bone, a vessel formed from the earth:

1. When God formed Eve, Adam said, "This is now bone of my bones and flesh of my flesh; she shall be called 'woman,' for she was taken out of man" (Gen 2:23).

2. In Genesis 3:19, God said to Adam, "By the sweat of your brow you will eat your food until you return to the ground, since from it you were taken; for dust you are and to dust you will return."

3. In Genesis 6:3, the Lord says, "My Spirit will not contend with humans forever, for they are mortal; their days will be a hundred and twenty years."

These images of temporary flesh and bone are not the descriptions one would expect from the Designer, especially when the issue of a self-portrait is in question.

Furthermore, throughout Scripture, we read of the torture and brutality suffered by those who called themselves Christians. Consider this passage from Hebrews: "There were others who were tortured, refusing to be released. ... Some faced jeers and flogging, and even chains and imprisonment. They were put to death by stoning; they were sawed in two; they were killed by the sword. They went about in sheepskins and goatskins, destitute, persecuted and mistreated" (Heb 11:35–37).

If these Christians' bodies were the images of God, why were they so willing to sacrifice them to persecution, torture, and death? God's people treated holy objects like the ark of the covenant, the staff of Aaron, and the bronze snake post with great care and reverence. If Christ's followers were also regarded as holy temples of God's Spirit, wouldn't they treat their bodies with reverence as well?

Hebrews goes on to say that the sacrifice of these believers was motivated by their pure love of God. It seems that if the human body is made in the image and likeness of God, He would want us to treat His image with the utmost care and respect, regardless of our love for Him. Yet consider the motivation and sacrifice of God's own Son: "Since the children have flesh and blood, [Jesus] too shared in their humanity so that by his death he might break the power of him who holds the power of death— that is, the devil—and free those who all their lives were held in slavery by their fear of death" (Heb 2:14–16).

Christ was made a little lower than the angels when He took on human form to suffer and die as the ultimate sacrifice for sin. As Hebrews 2:6–7 states, "What is mankind that you are mindful of them, a son of man that you care for him? You made them a little lower than the angels; you crowned them with glory and honor." A parallel passage, Psalm 8:5, likewise says, "You have made them a little lower than the angels and crowned them with glory and honor."

Christ did not elevate His stature when He took on a human body; rather, the incarnation was a descent that made Him even lower than the angels. If He came to earth and lived as a perfect man in the image of God, would it not have been the other way around? Would not He, in the flesh, have been exalted above

His creation? Yet in God's redemptive plan, Jesus "made himself nothing by taking the very nature of a servant" (Phil 2:7). In the ultimate paradox, God, who created humanity in His own image, sent His Son to earth in "human likeness" (Phil 2:7), and this divine man "*humbled* himself by becoming obedient to death— even death on a cross" (Phil 2:8).

Hebrews 1:3-4 reveals the victory that flowed from such an amazing sacrifice: "After he had provided purification for sins, he sat down at the right hand of the Majesty in heaven. So he became as much superior to the angels as the name he has inherited is superior to theirs." Christ, who took on human flesh and placed Himself below the heavenly beings He had created, was exalted in the end, raised once more above the angels in honor and glory. Understanding the significance of the incarnation of Christ and God's redemptive purpose in creation is essential to understanding the image of God.

UNDERSTANDING REDEMPTION

Over and over in Scripture, we see a clear distinction between flesh and blood and the soul. The person (or soul) who inhabits a human body is known and loved by God. It is that person Christ died for. The body is formed, lives for up to 120 years, and then dies—a mere mist in the scope of eternity. It is the soul that God grants eternal life through Christ's sacrifice. The apostle Paul wrote, "For we live by faith, not by sight. We are confident, I say, and would prefer to be away from the body and at home with the Lord. So we make it our goal to please him, whether we are at home in the body or away from it. For we must all appear before the judgment seat of Christ, so that each of us may receive what is due us for the things done while in the body, whether good or bad" (2 Cor 5:7-10).

Clearly, the body is a vessel that we as persons inhabit. It is an earthly biomachine for our soul. If the legs work, we should use them to carry the message of God's love throughout the world. If the arms work, we should use them to minister to those in need. If the tongue works, we should use it to speak truth of the gospel and praise our Father in heaven. The body is not our final form. It is a means to an end—a temporary and necessary tool for doing the work of God in the physical world. Yet we must still answer this question: Is the body designed in the image of God?

One could make the case that the human body and the soul that dwells within it are both shaped in the likeness of God. Our physical and spiritual traits are the aspects that separate us from all of creation. The human body is so complex that we have not yet begun to fully explore its depths. That complexity is symbolic of the very nature of God.

In Habakkuk 1:5, God declares, "Look at the nations and watch—and be utterly amazed. For I am going to do something in your days that you would not believe, even if you were told." This declaration foreshadowed the outpouring of God's power in the human soul through the Holy Spirit. Humanity reflects the true image of God when the soul is coupled with God's Spirit. The image of God is the personhood of the individual, who has been granted sonship by faith in Christ (Gal 3:26). It is the one who cries "Abba, Father."

The sons and daughters of the Most High, whose names are written in the Book of Life, are the ones who are truly made in the image of God. The body we have been given on this earth is a tribute to His creativity, a gift during our time here. Our ability to choose—to make either good or bad decisions—is a freedom we have been granted, but we reflect the image and likeness of God when we love holiness and morality. The transformed soul makes decisions and directs the body to follow a course that honors the Lord.

Romans 12:2 reminds those who bear God's image, "Do not conform to the pattern of this world, but be transformed by the renewing of your mind. Then you will be able to test and approve what God's will is—his good, pleasing and perfect will." Both the decisions of our minds and the actions of our bodies are subject to souls that are transformed into the likeness of Christ. This is expressed in 2 Corinthians 3:18: "And we all, who with unveiled faces contemplate the Lord's glory, are being transformed into his image with ever-increasing glory, which comes from the Lord, who is the Spirit."

God breathed the Holy Spirit and all of His characteristics (Gal 5:16–26) into Adam and Eve when He created them. But the indwelling Spirit was lost when Adam and Eve disobeyed. The Scriptures tell us that "Then the LORD God formed a man from the dust of the ground and breathed into his nostrils the breath of life, and the man became a living being" (Gen 2:7). God did not breathe into the nostrils of all the living creatures, so what was the difference? Life was all around Adam, so what was the "breath of life" God instilled in man? It was the Spirit of God. He was in Adam and Eve at the beginning, but He departed when they chose evil and allowed sin to corrupt the perfection that was required for the Spirit of God to dwell within them.

It took another 4,000 years before the sacrifice of Jesus Christ offered a way for humankind to be filled with His Spirit once again. The Spirit, who had not dwelt in the human heart since the fall, was poured out after the resurrection when Jesus breathed on His disciples and said, "Peace be with you! As the Father has sent me, I am sending you. ... Receive the Holy Spirit" (John 20:21–22).

We must not forget that Jesus is the living Word of God, and He was "with God in the beginning" (John 1:1–2). This is why God said at creation, "Let us make mankind in *our image*" (Gen 1:26, emphasis added). Just as He gave the breath of life to Adam, God offers the breath of life to restore His image in those who have accepted the blood sacrifice of Jesus on their behalf. This acceptance of the blood reflects the Israelites' act of covering their doorposts in Egypt with the blood of sacrificial lambs to signify that they belonged to God (Exod 12:21–28; 1 Cor 5:7). Our bodies are now temples of the Holy Spirit (1 Cor 6:19; Eph 1:13–14) —as God initially designed us and always intended they should be.

This is the image of God. Through Christ, we can attain that which was lost and be the light in a dark world.

Let's recap these first two chapters. To understand prayer, you must first realize that there is a God in heaven and we are formed in His image. If we accept the gift of salvation (justified through faith in Jesus Christ), then we receive the Holy Spirit, empowering and enabling our prayers. You see, in Romans, we are given insight into the relationship of the Holy Spirit and God the Father, which enables our prayer life to function:

> In the same way, the Spirit helps us in our weakness. We do not know what we ought to pray for, but the Spirit himself intercedes for us through wordless groans. And he who searches our hearts knows the mind of the Spirit, because the Spirit intercedes for God's people in accordance with the will of God (Rom 8:26–28).

So you see, since we are temples of the Holy Spirit (which we will discuss more later on), we have an intercessor who takes our prayers to God the Father and even interprets them on our behalf. This is the communication line—and understanding this vital point is critical if you are to advance in your training. Carefully consider what I have shared thus far before reading further in this guide to spiritual warfare.

NATIONAL PRAYER

LUIS PALAU

Our Father and our God,

We thank you for the many blessings You have poured out on America, and we praise You for Your mercy.

You have said: "Righteousness exalts a nation, but sin condemns any people."[1] We confess, O Lord, our national and personal sins. We repent and ask forgiveness for all actions that dishonor You.

O God, bless our president and other leaders. Provide them with wisdom and move them to honor You.

Deliver this great nation from all our enemies as we recommit ourselves to trust, serve, and obey Your commands.

We pray in the name of our Lord and Savior, Jesus Christ,

Amen.

CHAPTER 3

ENLISTING: UNDERSTANDING PRAYER

JOHN BORNSCHEIN

To understand prayer is to conceptualize something that is far greater than human comprehension. Think for a moment about the universe, which contains more than one hundred billion galaxies, with more than one hundred billion stars per galaxy.[1] How can one explain that the God who created and holds in His hands such a vast universe (Job 37–39) can pause from all the demands for His attention to listen to, contemplate, and even act upon the petitions of human beings? Actually, it is not a matter of asking *how* God can pause to hear us pray, but *why*? Why would such a powerful and limitless entity, a force far greater than human words could ever describe, give ear to the thoughts and utterings of finite creatures—specks in such a grand and complex system? That is an exciting mystery in and of itself, and one that we will explore in this chapter.

But before we examine the strands of prayer that are woven throughout the tapestry of life, we must begin with a firm understanding that a satisfying prayer journey is only obtained in our desire for relationship with God.

The Creator has many names—Elohim, El Shaddai, Adonai, Jehovah, Theos, the Alpha and Omega. But according to the Bible, God is approachable and accessible through only one source: Jesus (or *Yeshua* in Hebrew). If you have not accepted the blood of Christ as the atonement for your sins, you cannot experience the fullness of relationship with God the Father through prayer. But the moment you receive God's gift of salvation, you are no longer a simple human. Rather, you become a child of the living God. This amazing transformation is described in the book of John: "Yet to all who did receive [Jesus], to those who believed in his name, he gave the right to become children of God" (John 1:12). Like a caterpillar in a cocoon that passes through metamorphosis and becomes a butterfly, so you, too, through new birth in Christ, transform from the dust of the earth, from the old nature, into a new creation—that which is eternal (2 Cor 5:17-21; Rev 21). It is our identity in Christ that makes the dialogue of prayer possible.

DEFINING PRAYER

Jennifer Kennedy Dean states, "Prayer is an interchange of love between the Father and His child. That desire you feel to pray is His love drawing you to delight in Him. You only need to respond."[2] For true Christians, prayer (*proseuche* in Greek) is "communion with God." It is the medium of divine revelation. Through prayer, we actually experience relationship with God. The quality of our prayer life then determines the quality of our relationship with God.

Prayer is talking with God and listening to Him, and it is enjoying the presence of God. In his book *Prayer on Fire*, Fred Hartley describes prayer as "what we do. It is our initiative to meet God, whether we are asking for favors, singing in celebration, or crying out in distress. Regardless of what shape or size it comes in, prayer is our effort to engage God."[3] Prayer can take many forms, including worship, confession, thanksgiving, praise, petition (asking for what we need and desire), waiting (silent listening and sensing of God), and warfare (command).[4] As believers, we can pray in the Spirit—even in language that may be unknown to us but is fully known to God (1 Cor 14:2, 27–28).

Our goal through prayer must be to know God better, to experience the fullness of relationship with Him. Through prayer, we honor Him. We give something back to the Almighty, something He desires greatly. God reveals Himself to us in the "prayer closet"—a quiet place where we cannot be distracted in our time with Him. As the book of Jeremiah notes, God will make Himself known to us: "Call to Me, and I will answer you, and show you great and mighty things, which you do not know" (Jer 33:3 NKJV).

If you do not desire to understand the deep things of God, if you do not desire to give praise to the Father, then the rest of this book will be of no use to you. Your mindset from this point on must be that you will no longer accept mediocrity in your life but will desire more in your relationship with God. You must be ready to break out of your ritualistic or traditional prayer practices, in which you may consider God as nothing more than a glorified genie in a bottle.

ABOVE ACTION

For years, I struggled with one-way dialogue in my prayer life. This was due to a narrow perspective of faith derived from works. In my mind, I lived by my religious to-do list, complete with check boxes: Go to church on Sunday, go to church on Wednesday, read the Scriptures once a year (with a morning or bedtime routine of following outlined chapters), go to men's groups, tithe every Sunday. Oh, and be sure to pray before every meal and at the close of the day. These disciplines, though healthy, were practices that demonstrated my commitment to the Christian walk. But they were my works, not expressions of love for my God and King.

I have been blessed to serve in ministry for more than 20 years. During that time, I noticed a common practice among the men in our church: They were often motivated to express their faith by *doing* something. As long as they were engaged in some activity, they were passionate about their faith. But their fire would begin to fade when conversations about God focused solely on emotional expressions of love for Him. It was quickly rekindled when a task needed to be done, especially if the project involved a group of men working with their hands to accomplish something in the community. Why did the fire return when they were engaged in a project? It was tangible; the objective was clear, and the goal was attainable. Rather than simply talking about some abstract inner change, they were able to demonstrate the change in a practical and concrete way, doing something they considered to be "kingdom work."

There is nothing wrong with men or women expressing their faith and love for the Lord through works. After all, we were "created in Christ Jesus to do good works, which God prepared in advance for us to do" (Eph 2:10). But prayer is often lumped into the category of intangibles and, as such, it receives little emphasis.

In the past, it was easy for me to get caught up in tasks because I felt that viable, daily disciplines pleased God. These things came quite naturally to me as a man. Prayer, however, was nothing more than talking into the air for a set period of time—but at least I was able to check that task off my to-do list at the end of the day. Another accomplishment recorded in the books!

It is this focus on works that is the foundation of all religion. Yet throughout Scripture, we find that God desires more than religion; He wants relationship. Jesus calls out to each of us, "Here I am! I stand at the door and knock. If anyone hears my voice and opens the door, I will come in and eat with that person, and they with me" (Rev 3:20).

My prayer journey took another step when I began to understand that there was a living God on the other end of the conversation. My words were, in fact, rising above the ceiling and reaching heaven. But I still did not fully grasp what prayer was intended to do. I am ashamed to say that it wasn't until recently that I finally began to comprehend the idea that praying is not about what God can do for me; it is about offering myself to Him, surrendering my own agenda, and seeking His glory instead. If we fail to cry out to Him, to praise Him, the rocks *will* (Luke 19:40). I don't know about you, but I don't want rocks taking my place worshiping the Creator of the universe or fulfilling the purpose He intended for me.

BUILDING A RELATIONSHIP

God desires relationship, but for many years I was preoccupied with works. Not only that, I was preoccupied with self. When I prayed, it was a preconceived line of thought followed by a list of needs, and I was often impatient for results. In my mind, God needed to provide fast results, and if one prayer was not sufficient, I took measures into my own hands. Hey, at least I gave God a chance to perform, and then I did what any good Christian should do, right? But I was still missing the point.

The apostle Paul tells us in Philippians,

> [For my determined purpose is] that I may know Him [that I may progressively become more deeply and intimately acquainted with Him, perceiving and recognizing and understanding the wonders of His Person more strongly and more clearly], and that I may in that same way come to know the power outflowing from His resurrection [which it exerts over believers], and that I may so share His sufferings as to be continually transformed [in spirit into His likeness even] to His death (Phil 3:10 AMP).

And in Ephesians 1:17, he wrote, "I keep asking that the God of our Lord Jesus Christ, the glorious Father, may give you the Spirit of wisdom and revelation, so that you may know him better." Paul got it. And he wasn't alone. Enoch, the great-grandfather of Noah, had such a deep relationship with God that one day God just took him to heaven (Gen 5:22–23). Later, Elijah, who lived every day in wholehearted devotion to the Father, was escorted to heaven in a chariot of fire. That must have been an incredible sight.

Throughout time, God has opened Himself up to men and women to initiate friendship. Friends with the Almighty—what a concept! In *Ten Prayers God Always Says Yes To*, DeStefano states,

> The fact is that we have a God who loves to commu-
> nicate. And the reason is that communication is the
> starting point for any relationship. Everyone has heard
> it said that God wants to be able to have a relationship
> with us. There is no truer point in all theology. Indeed,
> the thrust of God's communication with mankind over
> the course of history has always been relational and
> not conceptual. That's why he actually prefers it when
> we come to have faith in him through prayer, instead
> of through logical arguments alone. God doesn't just
> want to satisfy a curiosity we have, He wants to enter
> into a friendship with us.[5]

God called King David, arguably one of the greatest kings who ever reigned on the earth, a man after His own heart. David poured out his love, respect, and humility before God throughout the Psalms. In Psalm 63:1, David expressed his thirst for the living God: "You, God, you are my God, earnestly I seek you; I thirst for you, my whole being longs for you, in a dry and parched land where there is no water." God designed us to thirst for Him. Many try to quench this thirst by pursuing physical desires, but this is a hopeless quest with no resolution. As Jesus said, "Everyone who drinks [natural] water will be thirsty again, but whoever drinks the water I give them will never thirst. Indeed, the water I give them will become in them a spring of water welling up to eternal life" (John 4:13–14).

If you knew that ours was the last generation before the coming of Christ, how would you live? When you stand before the throne of God, will you know Him intimately as your friend, or will you be a stranger? Are you going through the routine of your Christian walk without experiencing friendship with Elohim? Through Spirit-led prayer, your eyes will be opened, and you will have an indescribable relationship with God that is rich and fulfilling.

In *Experiencing Prayer with Jesus,* Dr. Henry Blackaby writes, "How deep is your relationship with the Lord as you pray? Do you pour your heart out to Him with complete confidence and trust in His help, because you've come to know and experience His love? It takes time, like any relationship. The more time you spend with Him, the more you'll come to understand His ways, His heart, and His will as you pray."[6] It is my hope that when you have completed this study, you will never view prayer the same way again, and you will experience true intimacy with the Almighty each time you fall to your knees, clasp your hands, and speak before the throne of the Most High.

THE BASICS OF PRAYER

At the National Day of Prayer Task Force, we developed a simple PRAY acrostic to help people remember the basic elements of prayer:[7]

Praise

Repent

Ask

Yield

Before we request anything of the Father, we worship Him with heartfelt words of praise. (If you need help in this area, select a psalm from the Bible and read it to the Lord.) In her book *Certain Peace in Uncertain Times*, Shirley Dobson writes, "He invites us into conversation with Him because it brings Him pleasure. That's sometimes a little hard to believe, isn't it? The holy and perfect and all-powerful ruler of the universe enjoys our prayers of praise? But the proof is in the Scripture: 'The prayer of the upright is His delight' (Prov 15:8 NKJV). God actually delights in and pursues our worship."[8]

In Matthew, Christ provides a model of prayer for His followers:

> When you pray, go into your room, close the door and pray to your Father, who is unseen. ... And when you pray, do not keep on babbling like pagans, for they think they will be heard because of their many words. Do not be like them, for your Father knows what you need before you ask him.
>
> This, then, is how you should pray:
>
> > "Our Father in heaven,
> > hallowed be your name,
> > your kingdom come,
> > your will be done,
> >   on earth as it is in heaven.
> > Give us today our daily bread.
> > And forgive us our debts,
> >   as we also have forgiven our debtors.
> > And lead us not into temptation,
> >   but deliver us from the evil one" (Matt 6:6–13).

With this very powerful prayer, Jesus made sure we would cover the essential points in our conversation with the King. We *praise* Him, for He alone is worthy to be praised. We *repent* of sin, asking forgiveness so that nothing will hinder us from receiving the blessing of response. We then *ask* for those things we need and *yield* to His will, for He alone knows how best to respond to our petitions.

As we grow in our relationship with the Father, we will understand more clearly how to pray according to His will. Read again these words of James: "When you ask, you do not receive, because you ask with wrong motives, that you may spend what you get on your pleasures" (Jas 4:3). When we are focused on our own desires, we aren't praying with God's will in mind. James points out that one reason God doesn't answer our prayers is that our motives are self-centered and wrong. But when we *yield* our desires to Him, we find true contentment, receiving with grateful hearts whatever God provides. As the apostle Paul states in 1 Timothy 6:8: "If we have food and clothing, we will be content with that."

Although Scripture tells us that we have whatever we ask in Jesus' name (John 16:23), God may say no to our requests and even allow us to go through suffering. The apostle Paul was well acquainted with suffering. In 2 Timothy, He offers these words to encourage us in the midst of our sorrow: "Join with me in suffering, like a good soldier of Christ Jesus" (2 Tim 2:3), and "Keep your head in all situations, endure hardship" (2 Tim 4:5). Peter also encouraged those who were suffering, writing, "Do not be surprised at the fiery ordeal that has come on you to test you. ... But rejoice inasmuch as you participate in the sufferings of Christ, so that you may be overjoyed when his glory is revealed" (1 Pet 4:12–13).

ETERNAL

E. M. Bounds dedicated countless years of his life to exploring the depth of prayer. In his writings on prayer, he states the following:

> The most important lesson we can learn is how to pray. Indeed, we must pray so that our prayers take hold of God. The man who has done the most and the best

praying is the most immortal, because prayers do not die. Perhaps the lips that uttered them are closed in death, or the heart that felt them may have ceased to beat, but the prayers live before God, and God's heart is set on them. Prayers outlive the lives of those who uttered them ... [they] outlive a generation, outlive an age, outlive a world.[9]

Bounds makes a life-changing point: Our bodies will age and die, but the prayers that leave our tongues are a blessing to the Father for all eternity.

Chapters 5 and 8 of Revelation describe the prayers of saints as golden bowls full of incense rising to God as a fragrant sacrifice. Some versions say that the incense is a sweet aroma to His nostrils. The text doesn't specify the age of the prayers, only that they were brought carefully into the throne room by the angels. We cannot see our prayers rising like incense to heaven or grasp their enduring quality, but our prayers are eternal. As Paul wrote, "So we fix our eyes not on what is seen, but on what is unseen, since what is seen is temporary, but what is unseen is eternal" (2 Cor 4:18). This concept is further illustrated in the tabernacle itself. The final stop before entering the holy of holies was the altar of incense. Exodus 30:1–10 describes the altar of incense that was placed alongside the lampstand and the table of showbread in the holy place, which symbolized the prayers of God's people. It was to be a special fragrance unto the Lord, reminding Israel to pray and assuring them that their prayers were sweet-smelling and received by God Almighty.

THREE WISHES

How do you pray? I used to treat God as though He was supposed to grant me three wishes when I prayed. My prayers were filled with "Do this," "Do that," "I need this," "I need that." Believe me; it is easy to pray this way. But when we do, we act like spoiled children, demanding the benefit of the relationship's power but failing to build the relationship. We perform our Christian duties, and then we list the things we need from God.

Are you throwing a short prayer His way before you eat, while stuck in traffic, or when you are looking for the best parking spot? Or are you actively pursuing a relationship with the Father through prayer? If you are a parent, what would you rather hear from the child you love? "Thanks for the food, you're neat, let's eat," or "I miss you. I really look forward to our time together. I long to be with you. I know you have everything worked out already, but I am worried about some things today. I need your help; I really blew it today. You told me what to do, but I still messed up. I will do better tomorrow. But I really need you to be with me, because I am weak. All I really want to do is make you happy. I love you so much. I want to know you more each and every day. Help me and please forgive me."

What is the difference between these two prayers? The heart. The purpose, the intent, and the respect are transparent. Prayer is not a fitful, short-lived exercise. It is not a voice crying unheard and unheeded in the silence. It is a voice that reaches God's ear. And it lives as long as that ear is open to holy pleas, as long as His heart is alive to holy things—and we know it always is.

A HOUSE OF PRAYER

God shapes the world by prayer. The more praying there is in the world, the better the world will be, and the mightier the forces against evil everywhere. Prayer, in one phase of its operation, is a disinfectant and a preventive. Prayer is God's settled and singular condition to further His Son's kingdom on earth (Matt 6:10). Therefore, the believer who is the most highly skilled in prayer will do the most for God. Men and women are to pray for the advancement of God's cause. The one who knows how to wield the power of prayer is the strong one, the holy one in Christ's kingdom. He or she is one of God's heroes, saints, servants, and agents.

Jesus tells believers, "Ask, and it shall be given you; seek, and ye shall find; knock, and it shall be opened unto you" (Matt 7:7 KJV). The strongest disciple in Christ's kingdom is the one who can knock the best. The secret of success in Christ's kingdom is the ability to pray.

NATIONAL PRAYER
BARRY C. BLACK

You have given us a great country and laws that promote humanity's dignity.

Help us to guard and protect our way of life with diligence and integrity.

Thank you for food, shelter, work, friendship, hope, grace, mercy, worship, and peace.

Remind us that Your blessings should be shared, and keep us from forgetting the lonely, the last, and the least.

Open our eyes so that we can see the strangers at our gates, the starving, the homeless, the fearful, and the dying.

Teach us how to extend the hand of friendship to the unwanted, matching our words with deeds of kindness.

We pray in Your strong name.

Amen.

CHAPTER 4

BASIC TRAINING: THE FULLNESS OF PRAYER

JOHN BORNSCHEIN

A t this point you should understand the basic premise of prayer: relationship with the Father. In prayer, we align our direction with God's will. If you have not done so already, you need to learn to balance your study of the Scriptures and your quiet time. God will reveal Himself to you through your diligent pursuit of Him. However, when you dedicate time to Him in prayer, it is there that He will unravel some of the mysteries of the gospel and give you wisdom to navigate and understand the deep things of His holy nature. This is where the relationship develops. It is an awesome experience when you dive into the waters of truth.

So, how do we begin to experience the fullness of prayer—the deeper understanding of its purpose? Throughout Scripture, we are reminded to petition the Father with our requests.

In Matthew 18:19-20, Jesus tells His disciples, "If two of you on earth agree about anything they ask for, it will be done for them by my Father in heaven. For where two or three gather in my name, there am I with them."

These verses provide the fundamentals of experiencing the fullness of prayer:

- "I will proclaim the LORD's decree. ... *Ask me*, and I will make the nations your inheritance" (Psa 2:7-8, emphasis added).

- "*Ask me* of things to come concerning my sons, and concerning the work of my hands command ye me" (Isa 45:11 KJV, emphasis added).

- "*Call to me* and I will answer you and tell you great and unsearchable things you do not know" (Jer 33:3, emphasis added).

- "You may *ask me for anything in my name*, and I will do it" (John 14:14, emphasis added).

- "You do not have *because you do not ask God*. When you ask, you do not receive, because you ask with wrong motives, that you may spend what you get on your pleasures" (Jas 4:2-3, emphasis added).

The common point in all these verses is this: We have to ask in order to receive. That is not too difficult to remember, and it might be how we spend the most of our prayer time. However, asking goes deeper than this. God wants to give to us and care for us (Matt 6:28-33; Luke 11:11-13). It is in His nature as our Father; after all, we are His children. We just need to remind ourselves that it is about relationship, not privilege. Our hearts are not in the right place if we simply call on the Lord for answers to prayer without desiring to know Him as our Father (Isa 29:13).

DEFYING TIME

Here is a thought that may rock your very foundation. In 1905, Albert Einstein first proposed his theory of special relativity, which relates to the speed of light in relation to objects at rest. Five years later, he introduced general relativity, which "demonstrates that time is [inextricably] linked ... to matter and space, and thus the dimensions of time, space, and matter constitute ... a continuum."[1]

According to the theory of special relativity, two people observing the same event in the same way could perceive the singular event occurring at two different times, depending upon their distance from the event in question. What accounts for this difference is the time it takes for light to travel through space. Since light travels at a finite and ever-constant speed, an observer from a more distant point will perceive an event as occurring later in time; however, the event is "actually" occurring at the same instant in time. Thus, time is dependent on space.[2]

On September 10, 2008, the Large Hadron Collider (LHC), which is located in an underground tunnel on the Franco-Swiss border between the Jura Mountains and the Alps near Geneva, Switzerland, circulated its first particle beams. The LHC was built by the European Organization for Nuclear Research (CERN) at a cost of nearly five billion dollars. It is the world's largest and highest-energy particle accelerator, intended to collide opposing beams of protons with very high kinetic energy. Its main purpose is to explore the validity and limitations of the current theoretical picture for particle physics.[3] However, it may also be the means for unlocking the string theory, which suggests that there are 11 dimensions in the universe—not just four, as Einstein had theorized. The very concept predicts that an intelligent force could travel through space and time and be in a million places at once, conducting a million conversations without time ever passing.

There are several things to consider here. First, it is incredible how capable the human mind is. What an amazing design, courtesy of God Himself! The brain can process and store more than 25 thousand books' worth of data[4]—more than the Library of Congress can store. But God will only allow people to learn and accomplish so much; we know this from the story of Babel, where men were building great and mighty things, including a tower to God (Gen 11). The LHC is really no different. However, it has enabled us to ask the questions, contemplate, and dwell on the idea that God, like the very concept of eternity, has no bounds. He is not limited to space and time. As the psalmist observed, "A thousand years in your sight are like a day that has just gone by, or like a watch in the night" (Psa 90:4). Peter echoed these words: "With the Lord a day is like a thousand years, and a thousand years are like a day" (2 Pet 3:8).

At a meeting of the Christian Leadership Alliance at Focus on the Family, physician and author Dr. Richard Swenson spoke on the subject of God in relation to space and time. He asked the audience, "Is it possible to pray today for something that affected yesterday? Space and time are no limits to God. If He knew you before He made you, He heard you before the words left your lips." Swenson wasn't encouraging the audience to pray for God to change the past; he was simply trying to get them to break out of their mental boxes and understand that the living God can pause and listen to our every word. He can think about our words and determine if and when He should act upon our request. He is able to do this for millions of people at the same time; He could spend a million years thinking about our prayers, and not one second would go by for humanity. Is that not a mind buster?

David seemed to understand that God was not bound by time and space when he wrote, "All the days ordained for me were written in your book before one of them came to be" (Psa 139:16). When you pray, your conversation with God has no bounds. It even breaks the limits of space and time. In the words of E. M. Bounds, "Prayer is the easiest and hardest of all things; the simplest and sublimest; the weakest and the most powerful; its results lie outside the range of human possibilities—they are limited only by the omnipotence of God."[5]

LIBERATING THE PASSION

Prayer is an act of submission. Remember, praying is not about us; it is about what we give back to Him who first loved us. We may never see some of our prayers answered in our lifetime, but we must tarry with our Father. As Hosea the prophet said, "Let us press on to know the LORD" (Hos 6:3 NASB).

And prayer is simply an expression of faith. Prayer and a holy life are one and the same; they mutually act and react. Neither can survive alone, for the absence of one is the absence of the other. The deep things of God are learned only in prayer. Our whole being must be in our praying, just like John Knox when he declared, "Give me Scotland, or may I die." What passion Knox had for a piece of land!

Why do we often lack a passion for prayer? What holds us back? Our passion may be diminished because we are holding on to something that prevents us from communicating clearly with God. Or we may be harboring some sin we haven't confessed. Whatever may be at the root of our struggle with prayer, our Father knows exactly what is holding us back from experiencing the fullness of a relationship with Him. We need to confess it to the Lord so that nothing will interfere with our connection to Him (1 John 1:9).

The book of Hebrews encourages us to "throw off everything that hinders and the sin that so easily entangles. And let us run with perseverance the race marked out for us" (Heb 12:1). Instead of giving in to our weaknesses, sins, and failings, we must learn to pray "with all perseverance" (Eph 6:18 NKJV). Philip Henry said, "The best way to fight against sin [or any other struggle] is to fight it on our knees."

The Bible shows us repeatedly that one person can change the world through prayer:

- Elijah prayed for the rain to stop, and for over three years, it didn't rain (1 Kgs 17:1-7).

- Moses saved Israel from destruction by pleading with God (Num 14:13-19).

- Abraham's servant asked God to grant him success in his search for a wife for Isaac, and God led him to Rebekah (Gen 24:12-15). Isaac and Rebekah would give birth to Jacob, from whom the 12 tribes of Israel came.

God heard the prayers of these godly men, and He will hear our prayers, too. We have incredible power in prayer—far more than we can imagine.

ORIGIN OF THE POWER OF PRAYER

What power enables us to have a voice before God? In Genesis 6–9, God gave His covenant to Noah and spared his family from the devastating flood that came upon the earth because of sin. Noah was 10 generations removed from Adam (approximately 1,100 years). For 40 days and 40 nights, while the rains fell upon the earth, this covenant was preserved in a wooden ark made of cypress wood and covered in pitch.

Fast forward to the time of Moses, approximately 700 years after the flood. For 40 days and 40 nights (Exod 24:18), God gave His covenant to Moses and told Him to build a different ark. This ark was made of acacia wood, 3 ¾ feet long, 2 ¼ feet wide, and 2 ¼ feet tall, and covered in pure gold, both inside and out. It also featured cherubim facing each other, looking toward the cover. The lid of the ark was called the atonement cover, a very symbolic foreshadowing. Three times in Exodus 25, God told to Moses to put His testimony (or covenant) in the ark (25:10-22). Inside the ark was a "gold jar of manna, Aaron's staff that had budded, and the stone tablets of the covenant" (Heb 9:4).

The ark contained God's presence and power, and the Israelites were able to accomplish great things when they respected His presence and followed His commands. They were afraid to go to battle without the ark leading the way before them. With it, they knew no foe could prevail against them. Wherever the Israelites went, they witnessed the power of God in the ark. Here are just a few examples of this power:

- It stopped the flow of a mighty river (Josh 3).

- It brought down the walls of cities (Josh 6).

- It stopped the sun (Josh 10).

- It broke down idols and destroyed armies (1 Sam 5–6).

What was the source of the ark's power? The Holy Spirit (1 Kgs 8:27; Acts 7:44–45). This was the same Holy Spirit whom Christ said would come after His ascension (John 14:15–26; 16:5–15), the same Holy Spirit who inhabits those who have accepted the life-giving blood of Jesus. First Corinthians 6:19–20 says, "Do you not know that *your bodies are temples of the Holy Spirit*, who is in you, whom you have received from God? You are not your own; you were bought at a price. Therefore honor God with your bodies" (emphasis added; read also Eph 1:13–14). As believers in Christ, we are now temples of the Holy Spirit, whose power flows through us. What an incredible thought!

No wonder Jesus told His disciples, "If you have faith as small as a mustard seed, you can say to this mountain, 'Move from here to there,' and it will move. Nothing will be impossible for you" (Matt 17:20–21). This is referenced again in Matthew 21:21–22. If Jesus said it two times, we better take note. But remember, this kind of spirit can come out only by prayer (Mark 9:29). If the very power that was able to stop the sun dwells in your body, what is stopping you from taking the sword that belongs to you? You are the ark of the covenant on two legs. Your body is now gold in the eyes of the Lord, and the atonement covering is the blood of Christ.

Acts 2 describes the flames that rested on the heads of the apostles as they gathered to pray before the Holy Spirit came upon them. Just as the burning bush that Moses encountered in the desert radiated God's presence, the flames at Pentecost were manifestations of God's Spirit. Now, the Holy Spirit is free to dwell in believers by the blood of Christ, and God will give the Holy Spirit to all who ask (Luke 11:13).

An amazing transition occurred from the law to grace. Under the law, people demonstrated their love for God by their actions. Hebrews 11 lists the men and women in the Old Testament who acted upon their love for the Lord. But in the New Testament, you see a significant transition. Rather than focusing on actions alone, Christ began holding people accountable for their thoughts and the desires of their hearts. For example, in the Sermon on the Mount, He told those who gathered, "You have heard that it was said, 'You shall not commit adultery.' But I tell you that anyone who looks at a woman lustfully has already committed adultery with her in his heart" (Matt 5:27-28).

Why would Christ raise the standard of holiness? Because God wants those who have a relationship with Him to think and act like He does. Sin is sin, regardless of whether it is an action or a thought. Christ wants us to put off the old practices of our sinful nature and draw closer to Him. He wants us to love holiness as He does. And He enables us to do this by the power of the Holy Spirit.

Galatians 5:22-23 tells us that "the fruit *of the Spirit* is love, joy, peace, forbearance, kindness, goodness, faithfulness, gentleness and self-control" (emphasis added). The Holy Spirit produces *His fruit* in us; it is not fruit we grow in our own power or effort.

Under the law, people performed to prove their love for God and to earn His favor; now, under grace, we perform because we are already loved and forgiven. Our actions flow from our love for Him because we know that He accepts and loves us in Christ. And we are filled with His love through the power of the Spirit.

KNOW THE ONE YOU'RE PRAYING TO

Robert Murray McCheyne, a 19th-century Scottish preacher, wrote, "There is a constant tendency to omit *adoration* when I forget to Whom I am speaking, when I rush heedlessly into the presence of Jehovah without thought of His awful name and character. When I have little eyesight for his glory, and little admiration of His wonders, I have the native tendency of the heart to omit giving *thanks*, and yet it is specially commanded."[6] Even though Christ gave His life for us on the cross and calls us friends, and even His sons and daughters, we must remember that we are approaching a holy God who is receiving praise at this very moment from angels.

When Moses approached the burning bush, God said, "Do not come any closer. ... Take off your sandals, for the place where you are standing is holy ground" (Exod 3:5). When we go before the most powerful, most holy, most high God, we dare not go disrespectfully. We are also reminded of this in Ecclesiastes 5:2: "Do not be hasty in word or impulsive in thought to bring up a matter in the presence of God. For God is in heaven and you are on the earth; therefore let your words be few" (NASB). I've found that Revelation 4:5-11 and Ezekiel 1:26-28 also serve as regular reminders of where we are when we pray, as they provide a breathtaking illustration of God's throne and glory. Ezekiel describes his own response to God's glory:

> High above on the throne was a figure like that of a man. I saw that from what appeared to be his waist up he looked like glowing metal, as if full of fire, and that from there down he looked like fire; and brilliant light surrounded him. Like the appearance of a rainbow in the clouds on a rainy day, so was the radiance around him.
>
> This was the appearance of the likeness of the glory of the LORD. When I saw it, I fell facedown, and I heard the voice of one speaking (Ezek 1:26-28).

When I read these passages, I cannot help but come into God's presence with praise. In fact, worship seems to welcome in the presence of God and prepare our hearts to hear from Him, which is why Elisha wanted a harp before giving the prophecy of God in 2 Kings 3:15. I believe this is also why Jehoshaphat had worshipers lead the army of Israel into battle (2 Chr 20). I remember reading about General Patton having the chaplains make prayer a focus for the army, even personally cowriting the prayer cards for the soldiers. George Washington had a similar heart of reverence for divine providence. It seems that prayer and worship go hand in hand.

We must have our compasses aligned correctly so we know whom we are praying to and what He expects. We cannot determine our prayer walk by feelings alone.

Brian Toon, a distinguished former member of the National Prayer Committee, has told me many stories of his days flying in the US Navy. He was an F-14 Tomcat pilot and later became an air boss. Brian says that when pilots fly at night, they must adapt to watching and trusting their instruments and gauges. At night, a pilot can make several critical errors if he operates by his senses. In fact, the body will adjust so much that a pilot could be flying upside down and feel right side up. As the pilot pulls on the stick, thinking he is climbing in altitude, he actually flies straight into the ground.

The same is true when it comes to our spiritual lives. The apostle Paul said, "The person without the Spirit does not accept the things that come from the Spirit of God but considers them foolishness, and cannot understand them because they are discerned only through the Spirit" (1 Cor 2:14). If you think you understand spiritual things and know the One you're praying to, but you are not pursuing God's wisdom and direction through a balance of Scripture study and prayer, you may be off course. So stay focused and run the race to win the prize (1 Cor 9:24).

NATIONAL PRAYER

MAX LUCADO

Dear God,

Not to us, O Lord, but to You goes all the glory.

We depend on You. You give birth and breath and determine our days. You make every nation and set every boundary. We exist by Your power.

We exist for Your glory. Showcase Your power through this land. Display Your justice in our courts, wisdom in our governments, guidance in our schools and love in our homes.

Have mercy upon our sins. We have disrespected Your Word, disregarded Your gifts, discarded Your children. We are sorry. Forgive us, dear Father.

Grant strength to all our leaders. May they serve You first and honor You most. Remind us of the brevity of this life and the beauty of the next. Prepare our souls for the day we meet You in eternity.

This we pray in Your holy name,

Amen.

CHAPTER 5

ADVANCED TRAINING: SUSTAINING A RELATIONSHIP

JOHN BORNSCHEIN

Three aspects of prayer are essential to sustaining an ongoing relationship with the Father:

1. Pursue God's will from the moment you rise each morning, making it your sole mission to please Him.

2. Use your lips to praise God in worship and prayer.

3. Petition the Father regularly for the needs of others through intercessory prayer.

STARTING OUT THE DAY RIGHT

Martin Luther once said, "Work, work, from early until late. In fact, I have so much to do that I shall spend the first three hours in prayer." What a paradigm shift! Even now, as you read these words, you may be thinking about all the things that you need to accomplish. The tasks of the day can be overwhelming for many of us. It was no different for Martin Luther. But he knew he couldn't face the obstacles and challenges of the day without God's hand guiding him. Just being in the presence of the Lord for a moment of solitude at the beginning of each day can ease your burdens, renew your vision, and replenish the spiritual stores of wisdom you need to make decisions through the day.

When I first began praying every morning, I found it difficult to pray for even 10 minutes; now, I often find myself in prayer for hours. And I've since found that my day is more productive and my mind is better prepared when I commit my morning to prayer. The psalms offer ample evidence that King David understood this essential practice as well:

- "In the morning, LORD, you hear my voice; in the morning I lay my requests before you and wait expectantly" (Psa 5:3).

- "I will sing of your strength, in the morning I will sing of your love; for you are my fortress, my refuge in times of trouble" (Psa 59:16).

- "O God, You are my God; Early will I seek You" (Psa 63:1 NKJV).

- "But I cry to you for help, LORD; in the morning my prayer comes before you" (Psa 88:13).

William Wilberforce also spoke of the importance of regular prayer, early and often: "Of all things, guard against neglecting God in the prayer closet. There is nothing more fatal to the power of religion. More solitude and earlier hours—prayer three times a day, at least. How much better might I serve if I cultivated a closer communion with God!"[1]

If pleasing God is our only mission as we rise each morning, then pursuing Him in the morning shows respect and honor for the One who will direct our path throughout the day. If we start the day seeking God's will for our lives, then the rest will fall in line. We may encounter conflicts and difficulties throughout the day, but it will be much easier to maintain a godly perspective and make wise decisions if we have started our day with our eyes fixed on Jesus. When we open our hearts to God in this way, we won't be able to contain the outpouring of our affection and praise to Him.

USING YOUR LIPS

Scripture calls praise the "fruit" of our lips (Heb 13:15). With our lips, we glorify God, praise Him, and honor Him. The psalms often describe audible praise as well. For example, Psalm 63:3-4 states, "Because your love is better than life, my lips will glorify you. I will praise you as long as I live." Similarly, Psalm 66:2 calls the people to "sing out the honor of His name; Make His praise glorious" (NKJV).

When David sang and danced before the Lord, his wife reprimanded him (2 Sam 6:12-23). But David was spot on; he didn't need to be reserved in expressing his love for God and the works of His hands. David was so close to the Almighty, he was unable to contain his passion—he loved the Lord so much, he hired 4,000 worshipers to praise and worship God (1 Chr 23:5).

If you pray in silence most of the time, I would encourage you to have a conversation aloud with God. Find a place where you can have some privacy—perhaps a hillside or a private room—and where you will be free to worship and pray without the fear of being seen or heard. You may be surprised to discover that verbalizing your prayers enables you to open up to God in a way you've never experienced. Later on, you may not be concerned about privacy, but for now, find a place where only you and the Father can converse without interruption. Then talk to Him, literally. Use the lips and the tongue He gave you. God wants to hear from you!

If you prefer praying in silence, He will hear those prayers as well. Silent prayer can be just as powerful and effective as audible prayer. The point I am making is this: If God has given you lips, *use them* for His kingdom.

And remember, praise starts with the heart; what proceeds from our lips is an expression of the soul. In Matthew 12:34, Jesus said, "For the mouth speaks what the heart is full of." We can go through the motions of praising God with our lips but our hearts are cold and distant from God, our worship is only empty words. The Lord rebuked His people for this attitude, saying, "These people come near to me with their mouth and honor me with their lips, but their hearts are far from me" (Isa 29:13).

INTERCESSORY PRAYER

Intercessory prayer is petitioning the Father for the needs of others. Intercession is mentioned more than 80 times in Scripture. The Hebrew word for "intercession" is *paga*, which means "to light upon." The Greek equivalent, *entygchano*, refers to conversation with a king that involves supplication and intercession on behalf of another person. The Greek word *paracletos*, referring to "one who pleads another's cause before a judge," is most closely linked to intercession in the New Testament.

If we are to model ourselves after Christ, we must be willing to give ourselves to prayer and fasting. The power of our relationship with God will come through concentrated devotion to others and their well-being. Hebrews 9:15 states that "Christ is the mediator of a new covenant" and is seeking those who will intercede for others—those willing to stand in the gap. In Genesis 18:22-23, we read that Abraham stood before the Lord to intercede for Sodom. But the Masoretic Text says that *the Lord stood before Abraham* and asked him to intercede. According to tradition, servants stood in the presence of kings—not the other way around—so English translations of this passage often show Abraham standing before the Lord. This translation may be culturally accurate, but it prevents us from seeing the intercessory heart of our God. He is the one who stands in the gap, petitioning for mercy on behalf of humankind, despite our sin. In a sense, God is petitioning Himself on our behalf. The ultimate example of this is Jesus, who stood before God as our intercessor when He gave Himself for us on the cross.

God also stood in the gap to intercede for the Ninevites. He commanded Jonah to go to Nineveh and teach those lost men and women the truth so that they could be saved from God's judgment (Jonah 1:1-2). He wanted Jonah to be selfless and intercede for those who did not deserve it. God's heart always seeks to intercede for us.

In the same way, we are to be imitators of the Divine Mediator. Ephesians 5:1-2 says, "Follow God's example, therefore, as dearly loved children and walk in the way of love, just as Christ loved us and gave himself up for us as a fragrant offering and sacrifice to God." As children of the living God, we must have God's heart—a heart of mercy and perseverance. We have been given the power of the Holy Spirit so that we can cry out to Him in intercession for others: "The Spirit you received does not make you slaves, so that you live in fear again; rather, the Spirit you received brought about your adoption to sonship. And by him we cry, 'Abba, Father' " (Rom 8:15). In Greek, Christ refers to the Father as "the sending me Father," that He might intercede on behalf of those who were doomed to perish.

Moses, Elijah, Samuel, and Nehemiah all interceded on behalf of Israel, and God heard them. One of the greatest examples of intercession took place when Moses stood before God on behalf of Israel. In Exodus 32:10, God said, "Leave me alone so that my anger may burn against them [the Israelites] and that I may destroy them." But Moses did not give up. And because God had a relationship with Moses, He allowed Moses to state the case on behalf of the people. In Exodus 32:14, we read that "the LORD relented and did not bring on his people the disaster he had threatened."

The account doesn't end there. Later, "Moses went back to the LORD and said, 'Oh, what a great sin these people have committed! They have made themselves gods of gold. But now, please forgive their sin—but if not, then blot me out of the book you have written' " (Exod 32:31–32). What a model of intercession! Moses was willing to lose his eternal inheritance on behalf of his people. He was willing to die for them, despite their transgressions.

King David referred to this event later in Psalm 106:23: "So [God] said he would destroy them—had not Moses, his chosen one, stood in the breach before him to keep his wrath from destroying them." Like the Israelites, we deserve to die for our sin. But just as Moses interceded for them, so has Christ interceded for us.

Over and over again, God Himself seeks those who are willing to put themselves on the line on behalf of others, those who are willing to walk through the fire if needed. Isaiah 59:16 states, "[The Lord] saw that there was no one, he was appalled that there was no one to intervene." Similarly, Ezekiel 22:30 shows the Lord seeking an intercessor: "I looked for someone among [the Israelites] who would build up the wall and stand before me in the gap on behalf of the land so I would not have to destroy it, but I found no one."

Intercessory prayer is more than simply praying a few words on behalf of someone and then moving on to other requests, never praying for that person or concern again. Intercession is pouring out our hearts for others, taking on the burden of those who are going through a trial.

PRACTICING PERSISTENCE

First Thessalonians 5:17 tells us to "pray without ceasing" (NKJV). Christ gave us some great examples of this. As He was teaching His disciples to pray, He gave the following illustration:

> Which of you shall have a friend, and go to him at midnight and say to him, "Friend, lend me three loaves; for a friend of mine has come to me on his journey, and I have nothing to set before him"; and he will answer

from within and say, "Do not trouble me; the door is now shut, and my children are with me in bed; I cannot rise and give to you"? I say to you, though he will not rise and give to him because he is his friend, yet *because of his persistence* he will rise and give him as many as he needs.

So I say to you, ask, and it will be given to you; seek, and you will find; knock, and it will be opened to you (Luke 11:5–9 NKJV, emphasis added).

Sometime later, Jesus told His disciples the following parable:

"In a certain town there was a judge who neither feared God nor cared what people thought. And there was a widow in that town who kept coming to him with the plea, 'Grant me justice against my adversary.'

For some time he refused. But finally he said to himself, 'Even though I don't fear God or care what people think, yet *because this widow keeps bothering me*, I will see that she gets justice, so that she won't eventually come and attack me!'"

And the Lord said, "Listen to what the unjust judge says. *And will not God bring about justice for his chosen ones, who cry out to him day and night?* Will he keep putting them off? I tell you, he will see that they get justice, and quickly. However, when the Son of Man comes, will he find faith on the earth?" (Luke 18:2–8, emphasis added).

In Matthew 15:21–28, a Canaanite woman who pleaded with Jesus on behalf of her daughter exemplified this kind of intercession. After Jesus had begun to turn away from her after her first cry because she was not an Israelite, she persisted, kneeling before Him and saying, "Lord, help me!" (Matt 15:25). When Jesus responded by stating, "It is not right to take the children's bread and toss it to the dogs," she did not give up, but said "Yes it is, Lord ... even the dogs eat the crumbs that fall from their master's table" (Matt 15:26-27). And her persistence paid off; Matthew 15:28 records, "Then Jesus said to her, 'Woman, you have great faith! Your request is granted.' And her daughter was healed from at that moment."

These passages demonstrate the perseverance of those who interceded for others. Those who carried the burden of intercession did not give up. They petitioned with great passion and expectation for results. They had faith and were willing to go the distance.

DING-DONG-DITCH PRAYER

If you are praying for an issue in your life, do you just say one prayer and then move on without giving it another thought? I doubt it. Your burdens are very real to you. You want answers. You want results. So you are passionate about seeking resolution. But E. M. Bounds notes that impatience is often a cause of unanswered prayer. He states, "I think Christians fail so often to get answers to their prayers because they do not wait long enough on God. They just drop down and say a few words, and then jump up and forget it and expect God to answer them. Such praying always reminds me of the small boy ringing his neighbour's door-bell, and then running away as fast as he can go."[2]

When I heard that a brother in Christ with three small children at home had just been laid off from his job, I knew he was praying as he had never prayed before. He must have felt scared, vulnerable, and weak. He was right where God needed him to be—dependent on Him for answers.

When we are truly broken, God can reveal Himself and do what we could never do on our own. The problem is that when we get what we want, we often forget to give Him the glory for the answer—just like the people who did not return to thank Jesus after He had healed them.

ALIGNING OUR REQUESTS TO GOD'S WILL

My wife and I have five children. With three girls and two boys, I spend a lot of time in prayer. In addition to keeping our lives busy, they keep me in humble petition constantly. My wife has also been battling cancer for years. She was diagnosed with thyroid cancer in 1997, but it wasn't identified until it had spread beyond the thyroid and into her blood. The cancer metastasized into forms of blood cancer and was also found in her lungs and cervix. The outcome looked hopeless. During that time, I began praying as I had never prayed before.

Sadly, it is often only when tragedy strikes that we turn to the One who has been knocking on the door of our hearts the whole time. To this day, our family is still praying for my wife's healing and waiting for God to answer, but we have never given up hope. We also recognize that my wife is in a no-lose situation: Either I get to keep her and spend the rest of my life on earth with her, or she gets to start eternity with the Father earlier than I will. My prayers began to change as I started spending more time with God.

We often do not receive what we want because we do not ask; and when we ask, far too often we ask outside of God's will (Jas 4:2-3). And so we need to learn how to pray according to God's will. What does He want in every difficult situation? The only way to find out is to spend time with Him.

My intercession for my wife changed from just seeking her physical healing to asking God for His help to raise children who will bring honor to Him—children who will pass on a legacy of faith and be a light to the many generations to come. Now my desire is that the Lord would enable my wife and me to set a new standard for our family heritage. We did not inherit a legacy of faith from our families, but I want more than ever to pass a baton to our five children that will become a memorial stone for them and their children (Deut 6; Psa 78).

Our family has matured in our relationships with the Lord through this battle with cancer, and for that I am grateful.

The Scriptures remind us that we will experience hardships (John 16:33; Acts 14:22; 2 Tim 2:3; 4:5; Heb 11:12:7), but does that mean God turns a deaf ear to our petitions? Absolutely not! He often allows us to go through trials to refine our faith and bring us closer to Him.

If you are praying for a neighbor, a friend, a child, or even a stranger, the Holy Spirit will guide you in your intercession to focus on the areas that really need His intervention. Sometimes the need is crystal clear, but often there are other deep-rooted issues that need to be addressed by the Great Physician—God. We often focus on the symptoms and not on the issue causing the pain. This is where God does His greatest work in both the person praying and the individual being prayed for. When Moses prayed for Israel, I believe that God was working on him as much as He was working on Israel.

HE HEARS

At the National Day of Prayer Task Force, we truly believe that God hears the prayers of His people and stays His holy hand of judgment on our nation, even if it means diminished punishment in contrast to what we know we deserve. We believe the words of 2 Chronicles 7:14: "If my people, who are called by my name, will humble themselves and pray and seek my face and turn from their wicked ways, then will I hear from heaven, and I will forgive their sin and will heal their land."

God hears His people and responds. But here is the kicker: You may not see the answer to your prayers in your lifetime. Abraham waited 20 years (until he was around 100 years old) for the birth of Isaac in fulfillment of God's promise. The prophets declared the coming of the Messiah, but they did not see Him with their own eyes before they died.

Remember, God is not limited to space and time. He hears our every word and knows the right time to respond. But we have to be diligent in the battle as we pray on the front lines. As James states, "The prayer of a righteous person is powerful and effective" (Jas 5:16).

NATIONAL PRAYER

HENRY BLACKABY

Oh heavenly Father,

You have made Yourself known to us as a nation by Your mighty works throughout our history.

From the beginning, You have been with us, and through many wars and conflicts, Your right arm has saved us. We have been amazingly and graciously blessed.

Today, we confess our sin of not responding to Your right to rule in our lives and our nation. We have despised and rejected Your will while imposing our own, and are now fully under Your judgment. Draw us back to Yourself, that You may return to us once again. Without You we can do nothing. You have promised that if we honor You, You will once again honor us!

For Your honor and glory we pray,

Amen.

CHAPTER 6

RECRUIT TRAINING: THE INTERCESSOR

KATHY BRANZELL

I magine for a moment that you—just as you are right now—were given the ability to change the world. Not after seeking counseling for your weaknesses, getting a degree from a well-known seminary, working out and preparing with some strength training, but *you, right now*.

Imagine that you had the power to expose anything done in darkness with hidden intentions so that all could see (Matt 10:26). What if you had the authority to bless businesses and families as they were getting started or were struggling through difficult times (1 Thess 5:11)? Imagine that you had the ability to comfort and encourage, to embolden and bring healing to the hurting, the struggling, the weak, and the sick (Prov 16:24). What if you could strengthen the military (Isa 41:10) while restoring purity and honor to the church and the youth of America (2 Cor 6:4–6; 1 Tim 4:12)? Imagine that you had the gift to cast out evil in media and improve education, while joining with fellow believers in those fields to bring honor and glory to God as they worked with a mission-field mindset in their workplaces (Matt 10:8).

What if you had that kind of power? How would you use it? Would you use it? Or would you ignore it, forget you have it, or refuse to use it—even when you knew it would make a difference in the lives of people and in the kingdom of heaven? Of course not! Then why do we forget to pray? Why is prayer sometimes our last resort if it is our most powerful resource?

I was once asked why anyone would want to join the Prayer Movement. Have you watched the news or walked through a school yard lately? Have you gone to the movies? Are you aware that we are at war? Have you heard any statistics about the state of families or the church recently? If you work: How is business, your boss, or your stock portfolio? How do you feel about those who represent you in government? Is there really justice in America today, and do our courts make decisions that align with Scripture?

Beloved, I ask you this: Why would you not see the need or feel an intense desire to join the Prayer Movement? Where does your hope come from (Psa 121:1–8)?

GRASPING AUTHORITY

God has instilled His authority and His power in us through His Spirit, who dwells in us (1 Tim 1:7–8). His power and authority can change the world. It is beyond our comprehension. We were created as Christ's ambassadors (2 Cor 5:20) to represent Him as we walk through life and have dominion over His creation. We were made to talk with the Father about everything good and bad, exciting and scary, thanking Him for the things we encounter here that point us to Him and asking Him to deal with the things that do not.

You may be asking: How can I be meek, as those who shall inherit the earth (Matt 5:5), and stand with authority at the same time? Maybe we misunderstand the word "authority"; it may conjure up pictures of cruelty, pride, or lack of submission, or even stir up memories of someone who ruled over you with an authoritative personality. Let's take a look at a few of the definitions of "authority":

- the right or power to enforce rules or give orders
- the power to act on behalf of somebody else, or official permission to do something
- a source of reliable information on a subject

Authority is given to us—and all believers in Christ, under the reign of God as His children, His servants, and His missionaries here on earth—to go and show the entire world His power, love, mighty hand, wisdom, and grace (Mark 16:15). Authority is accountability within the church with mercy; it is teaching God's commands with compassion. It is not judging (Matt 7:1) but demonstrating wisdom from the grace that has been extended to us. We exhibit this not by being cowards but by standing up when fear is telling us to sit down, by advancing when weakness is telling us to retreat. It is the boldness that claims the power of Jesus Christ when the world threatens to crush us; it is fearing God's court more than being taken to court; it is being certain when everyone else doubts. That is the steadfastness that God grows in us when we sign up to be prayer warriors in the Prayer Movement.

Prayer warriors do not hide in foxholes. They do not forget their armor and weapons (Eph 6:13–18) against the evil one, but rather, they enforce the desires of the Commander of His armies, both in heaven and on earth. We must get on our faces before Almighty God and pray with confidence, conviction, and certainty that not only does He hear us, but He will also act upon what we ask in the name of His Son, Jesus Christ. How true is the statement, "You do not have because you do not ask God" (Jas 4:2)? As a friend of God's and not the world's, we ask with the motive "Your will, Lord, not mine. On earth as it is in heaven. By your strength and to your glory. That your will is fulfilled, that victory belongs to you."

WHAT'S HOLDING US BACK?

Jesus said in Luke 11:9, "So I say to you: Ask and it will be given to you; seek and you will find; knock and the door will be opened to you." Why don't we ask? Why don't we seek? Why do we fail to knock? What holds you back from joining the strongest army on earth?

What do you say when a friend comes to you with a problem or your children have a need? What do you do when you see a mother struggling with her children's misbehavior at a store? What is your response to a homeless man asking you for some spare change? What is your reaction when you hear of tragedy, a popular movie star spiraling down the road of destruction, or of corruption in a government or business office? Is your first response to pray for each person and situation, or do you somehow try to fix, dissect, analyze, judge, or even gossip and groan about the situation or person and then move on with your own life?

How do those responses create change? Is the world a better place when we complain?

This may seem like a lot of questions for a book that you turned to for answers, but questions can help you start at the beginning—to know where you stand and why. Many people do not pray for others for a variety of reasons, from "I have so many problems of my own that I can't even think about other people's problems" to "I am afraid I will pray for the wrong thing; I might not know the whole story or have all the facts" or "Will it hurt my witness if God does not do what I ask Him?" Or maybe you have so many things to do that you are just too busy. (Ron Wilson at Focus on the Family sees the word "busy" as an acronym for "being under Satan's yolk.")

What strongholds in our lives make us weak-willed instead of warriors? Here are a few.

Stronghold #1: I have too many problems of my own to worry about other people's problems.

First, consider Luke 12:25-26: "And which of you by being anxious can add a single cubit to his life's span? If then you cannot do even a very little thing, why do you worry about other matters?" (NASB). Worrying accomplishes nothing. It may even set you back with fatigue, illness, emotional outbursts, and more.

The Prayer Movement presses on; it does not experience setbacks. The very best way to get your mind off your own problems is to start praying for other people. Follow the words of 1 John 4:7: "Beloved, let us love one another, for love is from God; and everyone who loves is born of God and knows God" (NASB). Lifting others up will lift you up. Praying for others puts your own problems into perspective and sets your heart in the right place as you "love your neighbor as yourself." Nothing cures a pity party like praise.

Focusing on a mighty, immeasurable, all-powerful, loving God reminds us that we have an awesome Father who loves us and knows and wants what is best for us. He has all the answers and all the resources we need.

Stronghold #2: Doubt.

When we pray, it's easy to fall into doubt, to ask whether prayer will really help. James 1:6-8 addresses this very issue: "But when you ask, you must believe and not doubt, because the one who doubts is like a wave of the sea, blown and tossed by the wind. That person should not expect to receive anything from the Lord. Such a person is double-minded and unstable in all they do."

The next time you find yourself held back from praying fully by doubt, remember these words from Mark 11:23: "Truly I tell you, if anyone says to this mountain, 'Go, throw yourself into the sea,' and does not doubt in their heart but believes that what they say will happen, it will be done for them."

Stronghold #3: I might not have all the facts, and I am not sure what to pray for.

Don't be afraid that you do not know all the facts or that there might be more to the story; God has all the facts. As Romans 8:26 states, "In the same way, the Spirit helps us in our weakness. We do not know what we ought to pray for, but the Spirit himself intercedes for us through wordless groans."

When we pray with a pure heart, in God's will, we do not have to worry about praying for the wrong thing. God always does the right thing—the *best* thing. And the best thing we can do is pray. As James 1:5 states, "If any of you lacks wisdom, you should ask God, who gives generously to all without finding fault, and it will be given to you."

Stronghold #4: I just want to "fix" things when people come to me with their problems.

Love and compassion for others makes us desire to fix problems, or at least help with them. Rather than praying, your first reaction may be to leap into action using your resources and connections to try to fix other people's lives. Of course, trying to help other people solve their problems—with a pure heart and good intent—is kind, but jumping into action before you pray over people and their situation is kind of crazy.

God not only knows all the facts about a situation, He also has all the answers and resources for every single person on the face of this earth. As Luke 12:27-31 states:

> Consider how the wild flowers grow. They do not labor or spin. Yet I tell you, not even Solomon in all his splendor was dressed like one of these. If that is how God clothes the grass of the field, which is here today, and tomorrow is thrown into the fire, how much more will he clothe you—you of little faith! And do not set your heart on what you will eat or drink; do not worry about it. For the pagan world runs after all such things,

and your Father knows that you need them. But seek his kingdom, and these things will be given to you as well.

You and I do not have all the answers, but God does. So why would we go anywhere else but to Him?

As the president of a Christian ministry for educators, I receive hundreds of emails every day regarding personal and professional prayer requests. So how is it that days and weeks later, we receive praise and thanksgiving reports from our schools reporting resolution to thousands of problems? *Prayer!* Week after week, God has heard our prayers, and we rejoice with educators and schools across this nation as we hear how God has healed the sick, changed the troubled student, brought unity to a torn school, and talked sense into an intoxicated parent terrorizing a campus. Prayer has prompted God to fix broken systems, change the decisions of the corrupt, bring resources to impoverished districts, stop violence and tragedy, and increase success. God has answered so many prayers and worked so many miracles that there are too many to count. In my own strength and with my own resources, I could not have helped the thousands of people who have come to our ministry for help. But with God, all things are possible (Matt 19:26).

Stronghold #5: I don't really know this person.

God may prompt you to pray for a person who you have never met. It may be someone you see crying in a grocery store or a celebrity being chased around by the media. It may be a child in a picture or a government official whom you do not even agree with. It may be someone who was rude to you on the highway or a receptionist with a sweet smile and an energetic attitude. It may be a worker who never arrives on time or a military plane full of soldiers headed to the front lines of a war. But we do not need to know all the people we pray for—God already does. He knows us all through and through—"the very hairs of your head" (Luke 12:7)—every need, desire, hurt, fear, gift, and family member.

God knows everyone we pray for; He created them. Consider Psalm 139:1–4: "You have searched me, LORD, and you know me. You know when I sit and when I rise; you perceive my thoughts from afar. You discern my going out and my lying down; you are familiar with all my ways. Before a word is on my tongue you, LORD, know it completely." Nothing escapes His attention or gets past Him. He does not get distracted, nor can He be tricked or outsmarted.

Proverbs 21:30 says, "There is no wisdom, no insight, no plan that can succeed against the LORD." Our job is to just make sure that no prayer opportunity goes unprayed.

Stronghold #6: "Well, they got what they deserved."

Friends, what God's Word says is enough for me:

> The LORD is compassionate and gracious,
>   slow to anger, abounding in love.
> He will not always accuse,
>   nor will he harbor his anger forever;
> he does not treat us as our sins deserve
>   or repay us according to our iniquities.
> For as high as the heavens are above the earth,
>   so great is his love for those who fear him;
> as far as the east is from the west,
>   so far has he removed our transgressions from us
>   (Psa 103:8–12).

I thank God every day that He does not treat me as my sins deserve. How could I ever ask for His mercy for myself and His judgment for another? Instead, we should remember Luke 6:37, which states, "Do not judge, and you will not be judged. Do not condemn, and you will not be condemned. Forgive, and you will be forgiven."

I have been forgiven much, and therefore I will forgive much. I am human, and so are the rest of the people I walk this earth with. And as 1 Corinthians 4:3–5 states, "I care very little if I am judged by you or by any human court; indeed, I do not even judge myself. ... It is the Lord who judges me. Therefore judge nothing before the appointed time; wait until the Lord comes. He will bring to light what is hidden in darkness and will expose the motives of the heart" (1 Cor 4:3–5).

Who am I that He would love me, forgive me, and think loving thoughts toward me? Who am I that I would not want that for all of humankind? Second Peter 3:9 says, "The Lord is not slow in keeping his promise, as some understand slowness. Instead he is patient with you, not wanting anyone to perish, but everyone to come to repentance." Who am I not to desire the same?

Stronghold #7: Does God really expect me to pray for my "enemies"?

Throughout the Old Testament, God makes it clear that He desires people to pray on behalf of one another. For example, after God allowed Satan to afflict Job in an effort to shake his faith, Job's friends accused him of sin, increasing his suffering. Nevertheless, God instructed Job to pray over his friends so that He would not deal with them according to their folly (Job 42:7–9), and Job obeyed.

In 1 Kings 13, King Jeroboam stretched out his hand to harm the man of God sent to prophesy against him, and his hand shriveled up and could not be pulled back. The king then asked the man of God to pray for his hand to be restored. Jeroboam did not ask him to pray for his soul or for forgiveness, but as a sign of faith in God and God's glory, the prophet prayed for the evil king, and his hand was restored.

Jesus expressed that same wish in the New Testament: "You have heard that it was said, 'Love your neighbor and hate your enemy.' But I tell you, love your enemies and pray for those who persecute you, that you may be children of your Father in heaven" (Matt 5:43–44). And on the cross, Christ cried out for forgiveness for those who had plotted against Him, betrayed Him, and crucified Him. The example has been given; it is for us to follow.

These strongholds chain us down and hold us captive by the deceiver. Pray them away. Break their bonds with the supernatural power of God in you, implementing the freedom given to you by Christ on the cross.

ONWARD

The role of intercessor may seem mysterious to some and inefficient to others. How many times have you heard someone say, "Well, all we can do is pray"? I pray that by now you have begun to grasp the incredible power and profit that come through prayer alone. We are more than conquerors through Christ. If we expect to do anything to improve situations, circumstances, and souls, we must start with prayer. It is only in being still (Psa 46:10) in faith-filled prayer that we can move mountains.

Onward, Christian soldier! The Prayer Movement is on the move. It is about advancing the kingdom, taking a leap of faith. It is pressing on to finish the race. As a fellow member of the Prayer Movement, you *can* change the world.

NATIONAL PRAYER
CHARLES R. SWINDOLL

Almighty God,

We pause to reflect on Your character as we seek wisdom for such a time as this.

> In these unsafe days,
> You remain all-powerful and able to protect;
>
> In these uncertain times,
> You remain all-knowing, leading us aright;
>
> In the unprecedented events we're facing,
> You remain absolutely sovereign.

Our times are in Your hands.

Therefore, our dependence on You, is total, not partial
   ... our need for Your forgiveness is constant
       ... our gratitude for Your grace is profound
           ... our love for You is deep.

We ask that You guard and guide our president and all who serve the people of these United States. May uncompromising integrity mark their lives. We also ask that You unite us as truly "one nation, under God." May genuine humility return to our ranks. And may that blend of integrity and humility heal our land.

In our Lord's name we pray,

Amen.

CHAPTER 7

THE HOME FRONT: PRAYER AND THE FAMILY

ROBERT VELARDE

WITH JOHN BORNSCHEIN, ASHLEY BORNSCHEIN, LINDA RUTZEN, AND KARA SCHWAB

While the front lines can easily become our focus, we can't underestimate the importance of the home front—and corporate family prayer—in training up the next generation in faith. Family prayer is the power source from which that faith derives its life—families that pray together lay hold of the very power of God to cope with the challenges of daily living.

Prayer can be as dynamic and varied as your own imagination and creativity allow. Mealtime and bedtime are great starting points, but God has so much more in store for you as your family learns to talk to Him. Prayers can be spoken aloud, sung, staged, danced, or even painted. The possibilities are endless as you turn your family's heart toward the Lord. You'll want to begin a journal of requests in order to refresh your memory and jump-start your words of thanksgiving.

God wants your family to shine like lights in a rapidly darkening and dysfunctional world. He desires each member to have his or her eyes opened to realities that others refuse to see. He longs for you to walk with Christ through a larger, more wondrous world than some can imagine. So take off the roof—establish a direct link between your home and the heart of the King of all creation.

No greater or more crucial task has been entrusted to us as parents than that of teaching our children to pray.

THE FAMILY THAT PRAYS TOGETHER

Prayer is a matter of matching words and actions, recognizing that the battle is raging in our own backyards. A life of prayer is a committed life, a life lived consistently under the shadow cast by a bright but unseen light. True prayers are not merely said—they are lived and breathed. They spring out of the heart, bubble up through the soul, and find escape through a hundred different gateways of expression. We walk them as well as talk them. They are part of who we are in the Lord Jesus Christ.

Dr. Gary Smalley, in his book *Homes of Honor*, tells us that healthy families are distinguished by six unmistakable characteristics: The members have a high degree of appreciation for one another; they spend a great deal of time together; they communicate openly; they share a strong sense of mutual commitment; their common life is marked by a high degree of spiritual orientation; and they are able to deal with crisis in a positive, constructive manner. It seems to me that this profile perfectly describes the group dynamics of a family that regularly seeks God together—a family where mom, dad, sister, and brother share their needs and concerns with one another, vocalize their petitions together in prayer, and watch vigilantly for the Lord's answers. Talk about bonding! It's hard to imagine a surer method of building family solidarity.

Statistics on Americans Who Pray

- 88 percent pray
- 82 percent believe in the healing power of prayer
- 78 percent say prayer is an important part of daily life
- 63 percent pray often
- 25 percent pray occasionally
- 65 percent believe that they have had prayers answered specifically
- 79 percent say praying helps speed recovery
- 24 percent say they have been cured through prayer
- 49 percent have prayed for guidance in finances[1]

The majority of Americans have prayed for their families, but how many of them live lives of true prayer? Although 90 percent of Protestants and 88 percent of Catholics had prayed in the seven days before a Barna study,[2] only 9 percent of American adults said that prayer was their most fulfilling spiritual practice.[3]

Scripture Compels Us to Pray

- "The prayer of a righteous person is powerful and effective" (Jas 5:16).

- "Therefore we do not lose heart ... For our light and momentary troubles are achieving for us an eternal glory that far outweighs them all. So we fix our eyes not on what is seen, but on what is unseen, since what is seen is temporary, but what is unseen is eternal" (2 Cor 4:16–18).

- "'For I know the plans I have for you,' declares the LORD, 'plans to prosper you and not to harm you, plans to give you hope and a future. Then you will call on me and come and pray to me, and I will listen to you. You will seek

me and find me when you seek me with all your heart' "
(Jer 29:11-13).

- "If my people, who are called by my name, will humble
themselves and pray and seek my face and turn from
their wicked ways, then I will hear from heaven, and I will
forgive their sin and will heal their land" (2 Chr 7:14).

THE IMPACT OF A LIFE OF PRAYER

Before civil government existed, there were families. Before the
church was established to point people to God, there were families. The family is the basic building block of society. If the family is strong, the whole culture has a sturdy foundation. Today,
however, the American family is under attack—many elements
in our culture can break down the family's authority and stability. Never has there been a greater need to build up the entire
structure of the family. Prayer strengthens families and leaves a
lasting impact on the ones we love.

The following excerpts from various sources describe the life-
changing impact of prayer on families. Through them, you'll
see—there are battles to be fought even on the home front, and
prayer is our more important weapon.

Healing and Hope

In 1975, Ann was diagnosed with precancerous condition of
the cervix. Her cervix had scarred shut from a biopsy. In 1978,
she was diagnosed with Asherman's Syndrome (uterine walls
had grown together) and cervical stenosis (cervix completely
sealed). She related:

> They operated with lots of special equipment, includ-
> ing a laser, to try and correct the problems ... I was told
> I'd never have a baby ... Bob and I were visited by my
> brother Tom ... Tom and his wife laid their hands on
> me and prayed ... three or four weeks passed and I got

pregnant ... I never had a single problem during my pregnancy ... Bob and I had a baby girl, and we named her Kathryn. I remember crying when I heard my daughter cry.[4]

Hearing the Word

In the 1930s Stalin ordered the purge of all Bibles and all believers. In Stavropol, Russia, this order was carried out with a vengeance. Thousands of Bibles were confiscated and multitudes of believers were sent to the gulags where most died for being "enemies of the state." Years later a team when sent to Stavropol. The city's history wasn't known at the time. But when the team was having difficulty getting Bibles shipped from Moscow, someone mentioned the existence of a warehouse outside town where the original confiscated Bibles had been stored since Stalin's day.

After much prayer by the team, one member finally got up the courage to go up to the warehouse and ask the officials if the Bibles were still there. Sure enough, they were. Then he asked if they could be removed and distributed again to the people of Stavropol. The answer was "yes." The next day the team returned with a truck and several Russian helpers to load Bibles. One of the helpers was a young man—a skeptical, agnostic, hostile collegian who had come only for a day's wages. As they were loading Bibles, one member of the team noticed that the young man had disappeared. Eventually they found him in the corner of the warehouse weeping. He had slipped away hoping to take a Bible for himself. What he found inside shook him to the core. The inside page of the Bible he picked up had the handwritten signature of his grandmother! It was her personal Bible. Of the thousands of Bibles still left in the warehouse, he stole the very one belonging to his grandmother—a woman persecuted for her faith all her life.[5]

Guiding the Young

My husband's great-grandparents, Frank and Hattie Yadon, lived on a farm in a remote canyon near Twin Falls, Idaho, in the early part of the century. They had found the Lord during a visit from one of the itinerant preachers who came through the area about once a year. The rest of the time, Frank and Hattie depended upon God through daily prayers and intercession for all their needs, whether for provision of basic necessities, healing, catastrophes or spiritual refreshment. As they gathered around the dinner table for the evening meal, Hattie would look around at their six rowdy youngsters and pray, "Lord bless all of the preachers and missionaries around this table!" Five of those six children became either missionaries or preachers, and seventy years later, five generations of Godly families involved in ministries across the world are the result of Hattie's simple, faith-filled prayers.[6]

Living God's Miracles

Just after Alison Thompson's first birthday, doctors found a tumor the size of a grapefruit on her liver. No one thought she would survive. Her family prayed. Hard. So did her entire church congregation. Almost immediately, the youngster's tumor began shrinking to the size of a golf ball, and doctors surgically removed it.

Today Alison is 11, and the only signs of her ordeal are long scars crisscrossing her abdomen and a sacred collection of guardian angels hovering about the family's Bradenton home.

"What we went through wasn't a tragedy; it was a miracle," the youngster's mother, Teresa, said. "I really believe prayer played a large part in her recovery. I think it guided her doctors' hands and everything they did."[7]

Overcoming Obstacles

The year was 1942. My grandparents, Frank and Irene Wheeler, who were missionaries in China, had been under house arrest for five months during the Japanese occupation. A small window of time had opened up for them to leave, and the last boat out of Canton was getting ready to depart. As Frank, Irene and their 12-year-old son, David, waited to board, David, my father, noticed everyone else was wearing a yellow ribbon. Tugging on his father's sleeve, he whispered, "Dad, everybody has ribbons except us." Suddenly an official came up to Frank and announced, "Others can go. You can't go." Apparently the yellow ribbon had indicated that certain papers had been signed, and Frank hadn't known about it. As the terrible realization dawned that they were going to miss the last boat to freedom, Frank bowed his head in simple desperation and prayed, "Lord, if you've ever helped us, help us now." A few moments later an official put his hand on Frank's shoulder and said, "We have decided you can go." Grandpa, a pioneer of faith, was a true friend of God. He knew when he needed help the most, God would be there—and He was.[8]

TEACHING OUR CHILDREN TO PRAY

These are difficult days for the family. How do we create a safe environment for our kids? How do we protect them from the evil influences of a culture gone awry, a society cut loose from its moral and spiritual moorings? How do we proof them against drugs, alcohol, and premarital sex?

The answer isn't far to seek. It's waiting for us at home. And prayer is the key. Family prayer, family worship, family devotions—that's where we're going to find the hope, the security, the salvation we're seeking. Families that pray together don't just stay together. They lay hold of the very power of God and mold the generation that shapes the future.

Learning by Example

Whether they know it or not, our children are appealing to us today in the words of the disciples: "Teach us to pray!" It's their greatest need. Built into all of us is a longing to cry out to a Power greater than ourselves, to acknowledge our dependence upon God and to sense His love and care. I would suggest that even the youngest member of the family feels it at some time or another. How are we going to help our children fulfill this holy longing? How are we going to respond when they come asking, "Teach us to pray"? What will we teach them—is there a lesson plan handy? And how will they learn? (For starters, we've included some tips on praying with your family in the "Field Guide for Family Prayer" at the end of this book.)

Children learn by example. Remember Moses' exhortation to the children of Israel: "Impress [these principles and commandments] on your children. Talk about them when you sit at home and when you walk along the road, when you lie down and when you get up. Tie them as symbols on your hands and bind them on your foreheads. Write them on the doorframes of your houses and on your gates" (Deut 6:7–9). In other words, a brief bedtime prayer is not enough. A quick, formalized family devotion may be fine in its place, but it can't do the whole job. We must live our convictions and demonstrate our dependence upon the Lord day in and day out, from morning to night. Consciously model your faith in the reality of prayer. Never miss an opportunity to speak openly of your love for Jesus in front of your children or to refer to your need for His help in any given situation. This is where the first small seeds of spiritual understanding are sown. This is how genuine trust in God begins to grow in the heart of a child.

Children will learn from being in God's presence. As children are ushered into the presence of God and enabled to experience His grace and goodness for themselves, they will inevitably make it happen. We can model the attitude and the behavior; we can set the stage, create the mood, and invite the players to participate; we can do prayer with children in a hundred different ways. We can open a door, lead our families to the threshold, and point the way inside. But in the final analysis, we are always left in blessed dependence upon the glorious mystery of God's absolute sovereignty. He alone has the power to draw "all men"—and that includes our sons and daughters—to Himself. This is eminently an endeavor of which it must be said, "Unless the LORD builds the house, they labor in vain who build it" (Psa 127:1 NASB).

The need for prayer in a child's life is urgent. In fact, prayer is the heart of a spiritually healthy family. Let's take the challenge and teach kids to pray! The call is clear, and parents are positioned to respond as no one else can. In our eagerness to teach children, we need to make sure that they know God exists and wants to know them through a personal relationship. When you child is ready to be reconciled to God, do not neglect to share the ultimate prayer of salvation through Jesus Christ. Together, we can raise up a generation.

TEACHING TEENS THE POWER OF PRAYER

God gave parents the responsibility to talk with children about Him, to pray with them, and help them grow in their own faiths (Deut 6:4-7; Psa 78:1-8). When we talk with our teens about spiritual things, our honesty, patience, vulnerability, and willingness to make time for them can open the doors to the life in Christ we hope for them and the relationship God himself desires.

Shaping a Life of Prayer

Before the sun splashed its orange hue on the walls of the marble quarry, the stonecutters made their way to their latest assignment: to finish removing the promising slab of white marble without breaking it into smaller pieces. The stone's color was good, few blemishes could be detected, and it appeared to be of appropriate size.

Carefully, they removed the stone from the quarry; a buyer made an offer, and off it went. Still just a large slab of marble. Not much to look at.

The artist, however, burning with a vision, took hammer and chisel and began to transform the chunk of marble into a masterpiece of exquisite beauty and grace. From the formless rock, Michelangelo brought forth the majestic statue the world knows as *David*.

What does it take to transform us from our "formless slab" condition into the piece of art that God destined for our lives? God uses the chisel of prayer to form, shape, and smooth us into His workmanship. Different chisels work different purposes, but all of them work together to shape us.

Teenagers and adolescents, empowered with a thoroughly taught and well-practiced prayer life, can become modern-day heroes and heroines of the faith. Sculpted and polished by a close relationship with their Creator, they can have futures that are filled with boundless opportunities. A young person, fervently praying with the abandonment and fearless faith of youth, will truly accomplish incredible things for God throughout his or her life. In addition, having established a strong personal prayer life, your teen will have already begun a strong foundation for his or her future family. Teaching prayer to your teenager is your investment in the ongoing godly traditions of your family's faith, in the kingdom of God, and in the future of our nation and world!

Remember: More is caught than taught! A child who grows up hearing his parents pray, sees them on their knees calling out to God, and is familiar with the sounds and fragrance of prayer in the home, will be much more likely to develop a strong prayer life. Pray for and with your teenage. Watch it become second nature to them, as they, too, develop a life of prayer.

P.R.A.Y.

Let's look again at four tools—Praise, Repent, Ask, and Yield—which can bring about incredible change and growth in our lives (we covered these earlier, in chapter 3). Together, they blend to constitute the body of prayer, which enables us to be transformed. In talking to your teen about prayer, you can use these tools to help explain how prayer works.

Praise

This is the exciting part. When we worship God, we are moved from being self-centered to being God-centered. Praise moves us quickly into God's presence, where we are surrounded by His holiness, love, and peace. As we honor God, we confirm a relationship with Him, one of dependence yet full of power through His Holy Spirit.

Almighty God, You are worthy of my highest praise! ...

Repent

This is the serious part. We've all done things that are displeasing to God. Sin, or disobedience to God, builds an instant wall in our relationship with Him. To be intimate with Him, we must confess all ungodly thoughts, words, or deeds, sincerely and humbly telling God we are sorry. Then, resting in His forgiveness, we resolve with all of our hearts to turn away from our sin. We give Him our rags, and He washes away the darkness and hurt and gives us His riches.

Lord, I come before You with repentance for my sin and disobedience to You ...

Ask

This is the powerful part. We've moved into God's presence with praise and worship, and we've removed all obstacles between us and God. Now we can call upon Him with our needs and share the deepest secrets of our hearts. His Word promises that He'll listen and answer! In trouble? Afraid? Helpless? Sick? Stuck? Open your heart. Call on God. Ask Him for help. His ear is tuned specifically to the sound of your voice.

Heavenly Father, I know that You will answer me when I call upon You ...

Yield

This is the peaceful part. To yield means to let God be God. We know of His great love for us, so we have to trust Him when we pray, that His answers will be perfect for our circumstances. Yielding involves waiting and listening for God to "speak" to us— in a quiet prayer time, the still of the night, in our consciences during a time of hard decisions—any time! When our hearts are soft and surrendered to Him, He's able to guide the course of our lives, drawing us ever closer to Himself.

Loving God, I give myself wholly to You. Be the Lord of all of my life ...

Formless slabs of granite, soft impressionable human hearts— all have unlimited, spectacular potential when placed in the hands of a master artist. As you model a life of prayer, watch as God's destiny is fulfilled in your family and for generations to come.

PRAY THROUGH THE SCRIPTURES

The best place to start your family in prayer is the Bible. Nothing can address our needs or concerns like the Word of God. The leaders, churches, families, and forgotten of our nation desperately need our prayers. The daily decisions, temptations, loneliness, and pressures they face are often overwhelming. Please take the time to look up the following Scriptures and pray through them for your family. Meditate on the precious and powerful words of Scripture as you lift up your loved ones.

- Children will grow in wisdom and stature, and in favor with God and men (Luke 2:52).

- Parents and children will hunger for the Word of God (Psa 119:103).

- The fruit of the Spirit will be evident in our families (Gal 5:22–23).

- As families we will be "salt and light" in our neighborhoods and communities (Matt 5:13–16).

- Parents will raise their children, training and instructing them in the ways of the Lord (Eph 6:4; Deut 6:4–7).

- Your children won't succumb to peer pressure, but rather will set an example in speech, life, love, faith, and purity (1 Tim 4:12).

- Your family will honor God so He would make your paths straight (1 Tim 2:1, 2).

- You will have strength to live a life worthy of the Lord and conduct business accordingly (Psa 1:1-2).

- Your children will be strong, courageous, and set apart for God (Josh 1:7-8).

- In times of trouble your family would turn to the Lord for mercy (Isa 55:7).

Remember as you spend daily time in the Word to always pray for your family as you read and meditate on the Scriptures.

DRAW YOUR FAMILY TO GOD

In our prayers we admit reliance on God to face the many issues where we can find no other answers but in Him. He transforms hearts through prayers—and oh, how desperately we need to be transformed, to stand on God's firm foundation as we go forth into the battles in our lives. Let it begin in your heart—and in the heart of your family.

NATIONAL PRAYER
RAVI ZACHARIAS

Holy Father,

In a world where so many are hungry, You have given us food in abundance; in a world where so many are hurting, You offer to bind up our wounds; in a world where so many are lonely, You offer friendship to every heart; in a world longing for peace, You offer hope.

Yet we are so stubborn and resistant. Have mercy upon us, Lord. Our nation is at a crossroads this year; we look to you to be our strength and shield.

Please give us the guidance to elect one who will honor you and to respond to the wisdom from above so that our hope may be renewed and our blessings be treasured.

In Jesus' holy name,

Amen.

CHAPTER 8

BOOT CAMP: MOBILIZING THE CHURCH

DION ELMORE

Shortly after Jesus ascended into heaven, the early disciples made the trip back to Jerusalem to gather and wait. They knew that something was going to happen. Jesus had instructed them to wait for power. But what exactly did that mean? What kind of power? They had walked with Jesus, they had observed Him pray, and they had participated in the miracles that He worked. But they really didn't understand what was going to happen next.

In my own experience, I've learned the same lesson. When I don't know what to do next, I wait and pray. That's exactly what they did: They returned to the upper room, and, as Acts 1:14 puts it, "all continued with one accord in prayer and supplication" (NKJV).

Imagine being there with this ragtag assembly of fishermen, tax collectors, tradesmen, farmers, fathers, mothers, and religious leaders—a group of ordinary people who found themselves right in the middle of something extraordinary. They were just praying and waiting for God's promise, His Holy Spirit. Receiving power meant that their lives would be dramatically seized, forever changed, and radically redirected. Once hindered by fear, apprehension, and misunderstanding, this group would soon become a very powerful army of witnesses. Lives would be transformed and miracles would be performed. The news would spread rapidly, the gospel would be shared, and thousands upon thousands of new disciples would be added to the church every week.

MAINTAINING THE MAIN THINGS

In those early days, the disciples would be flooded with opportunities to participate in God's work and then to see instant results. No time to prepare, no time to reflect, no time to even think about what was happening to them. The Holy Spirit had fallen upon them. As they sought God's guidance and struggled to accommodate all of the growth, they settled on a very simple ministry plan. They pledged to keep focus on the main things. With determination, they set out to focus on four key areas. In Acts 2:42, these are outlined for us: They "devoted themselves to the apostles' teaching and to fellowship, to the breaking of bread and to prayer."

The apostles understood their priorities, and when challenged with waiting tables, they, in the wisdom of God, chose instead to focus on giving themselves continually "to prayer and the ministry of the word" (Acts 6:4). By maintaining their focus, they remained plugged in to God. As a result, they maintained an intentional focus that alerted them to the needs and opportunities around them.

STAYING ENGAGED WITH THE BASICS

It's all pretty basic, isn't it? We, the 21st-century church, can take a few lessons from the founders. As we mobilize the church of Jesus Christ today, what are we focusing on? What are the current trends in the church today? What are we busy doing? Let's compare our activities to the activities of the early disciples. Are we focused on teaching the Word of God? Are we in the business of developing intimate relationships and promoting fellowship among believers? Are we praying steadfast, continual prayer?

We may do those things, but how intentional and effective are we at accomplishing them? You see, the most basic things are the things we seem to become the most bored with. We need to be honest in our assessment before we can be effective. We should ask ourselves these questions:

- Are we *steadfastly* praying over every area of our churches' ministry?

- Are we *steadfastly* seeking God's direction?

- Are we *steadfastly* asking for His protection?

- Are we *steadfastly* praying against every stronghold of the enemy that God reveals to us?

The early church's use of the word "steadfastly" indicates that they believed it was not only important but *essential* to keep these fundamentals in place. The idea is to devote ourselves continually and diligently to these things. They understood that without the foundation of truth, relationship, and prayer, there could be no real lasting impact in the church or through the church. The world was against them, the devil was roaming about, and they had to seek wisdom and direction from the Lord.

Things really haven't changed. The foundations of a sound church are still the same. Every church that intends to be about God's business with power must attend to these basics continually. We are still resisting the devil and storming the gates of hell. And we still need wisdom and direction from the Lord.

BEGINNING WITH A BURDEN

A number of years ago, as I was praying about the possibility of planting a new church, I kept running into the first chapter of Nehemiah. Over and over, at conference after conference, speakers drew my attention to the same verse: Nehemiah 1:4. Eventually, that verse captured my focus and led me to understand that powerful ministry grows from a heart burdened to pray.

Let's take a look at Nehemiah 1:1-4:

> In the month of Kislev ... Hanani, one of my brothers, came from Judah with some other men, and I questioned them about the Jewish remnant that had survived the exile, and also about Jerusalem.
>
> They said to me, "Those who survived the exile and are back in the province are in great trouble and disgrace. The wall of Jerusalem is broken down, and its gates have been burned with fire."
>
> When I heard these things, I sat down and wept. For some days I mourned and fasted and prayed before the God of heaven.

Before he received the devastating news about the wall of Jerusalem, Nehemiah was doing quite well. But, as often happens, along came a burden from God. Nehemiah stopped what he was doing, listened, and then wept and mourned for many days. The Lord had captured his heart. Here's a principle worth remembering: A captured heart leads to compassionate prayer.

Every major work that God prepares for us, He also prepares *us* for. The problem is that the preparation process is often difficult. It's uncomfortable to ask God to break our hearts over the plight of people. But if we look through His eyes, we'll begin to see a tremendous need all around us—need that will compel us to pray. In every city, every neighborhood, there are people who are in captivity, ensnared by the world, tempted in their flesh, and blinded by the devil. They are in "great trouble and disgrace" (Neh 1:3).

If, like Nehemiah, God has captured our hearts and we are compelled to fervent prayer, what should we do next? What did Nehemiah do? He mobilized. Nehemiah began to prepare through prayer. He sought wisdom, prayed for favor, and began taking steps to follow God's prompting. Even though Nehemiah had never been to Jerusalem, the plight of the people became personal to him.

If we have been compelled to pray, then we will be mobilized into action. Let's assess the needs and plight of the people in the community in which we live. Is there a need for us, for our churches, to rise up together and pray? To mobilize and take action? To mount up an attack on the strongholds of our common enemies? To take back lost ground, and to build a wall of protection around those who are desperately in need? Of course there is.

PREPARATION FOR ACTION

The apostle Paul offers an illustration of the mobilized power of prayer to the early church in Corinth. Attempting to teach these early believers the effectiveness of intentional prayer, Paul instructs them that "the weapons of our warfare are not carnal but mighty in God for pulling down strongholds, casting down arguments and every high thing that exalts itself against the knowledge of God" (2 Cor 10:4 NKJV). The weapon of prayer is powerful and effective. It is a weapon that, when focused against the strongholds of bondage, sin, arguments, and arrogance, literally tears them apart.

The early church formulated its strategy and tactics based on their observations of the strongholds in people's lives. God would reveal strongholds, and they would pray against them. They realized that the "principalities and powers" that they battled against were extremely busy fortifying existing strongholds and continually beginning construction on new ones. They also realized that the weapons they possessed were mighty in God. They had the weaponry, but they were not very skilled when it came to planning and carrying out warfare in prayer. In order to become skilled, they needed training and practice.

DEVELOPING AND MOBILIZING PEOPLE IN THE CHURCH

When I first began working in ministry, I spent a lot of time trying to encourage God's people to pray, and I discovered that I had no power to place a burden of prayer within people. I knew that there was power in prayer, but I wasn't quite sure how to mobilize people to pray or how to get them to take action. I found relief when I read Ephesians 4, which teaches that a pastor's role is not to incite people to pray or ensure that they do pray; a pastor's role is simply to equip the people to serve while allowing the Holy Spirit to impart to them a heart to pray and the desire to serve.

Like a drill sergeant, pastors are given the role of equipping new recruits and giving them the tools they need to become effective soldiers. And we are definitely engaged in a war—a war against the world, the flesh, and the devil. All of us are drafted into the Lord's service, issued spiritual armor and weaponry, and given instruction in effective engagement.

Equipping saints is a daunting task. Imagine that you are a drill sergeant in the army who is responsible for preparing men and women for battle, for taking raw recruits and turning them into the best fighting force on the face of the earth. You would have the best resources at your disposal, the best weapons, and the best equipment, and you could have as many months as you need. But you only have 30 to 45 minutes, once a week, to train them. And, by the way, these soldiers may not show up every week—after all, they are pretty busy with their personal lives. Would you take the challenge?

That's exactly the challenge that pastors face. In a sense, they have devoted their lives to training a "volunteer" Christian army: men and women with every physical and spiritual resource at their disposal, equipped with the most powerful weapons in the universe, and against whom no effective weapons have ever been formed. These men and women are able to battle with every principality and power, no matter how ferocious. And their assault will make the foundations of the gates of hell tremble and the walls crumble. But pastors are expected to train their army in just 45 minutes a week, 52 Sundays each year, or as often as their troops choose to show up. (If that is every Sunday, that's still only 39 hours a year—less time than most people spend at their jobs each week.) Without the Holy Spirit's involvement, this would be an impossible task.

So how do we mobilize the church to pray? This may sound simplistic, but the most effective way that I've found is to pray for them to have a burden for prayer. Pray for the people. Pray for them to understand the resources that they have available. Pray for a burden like Nehemiah had. Pray that the Holy Spirit will teach and train them as your pastors do the work of equipping them. Pray that they would understand that prayer is the powerhouse of the church. Turn up the heat on the saints so they can turn up the heat against the world, the flesh, and the devil.

TURNING UP THE HEAT

Charles Spurgeon understood this principle well. *Our Daily Bread* shared this episode:

> Five young college students were spending a Sunday in London, so they went to hear the famed C. H. Spurgeon preach. While waiting for the doors to open, the students were greeted by a man who asked, "Gentlemen, let me show you around. Would you like to see the heating plant of this church?" They were not particularly interested, for it was a hot day in July. But they didn't want to offend the stranger, so they consented. The young men were taken down a stairway, a door was quietly opened, and their guide whispered, "This is our heating plant." Surprised, the students saw 700

people bowed in prayer, seeking a blessing on the service that was soon to begin in the auditorium above. Softly closing the door, the gentleman then introduced himself. It was none other than Charles Spurgeon.[1]

The term "boiler room prayer" was coined to describe the real power plant of a powerful, praying church. At the Metropolitan Tabernacle, where Spurgeon served as pastor, there were hundreds of praying saints in the "boiler room" crying out to God during every service. They prayed for salvation to come, for freedom from bondage, and for power over sin. And God answered their prayer. They prayed for their pastor—that God would empower him and use him in a mighty way. And God answered their prayer. Faithfully, week after week, they prayed for the young men who were training at the Pastor's College and serving at that church and others that they were supporting. And God answered their prayer.

I had the privilege of sitting next to Rick Warren, a best-selling author and pastor, at a dinner a couple of years ago. We were talking about spiritual heritage, and he shared with me that his great-grandfather was one of those young men trained at the Pastor's College in London. He was sent to the United States and became a circuit-riding preacher. Rick's father was also a pastor, and today Rick himself is an influential evangelical pastor. I believe that the prayers prayed by those "boiler room" saints over 100 years ago are still affecting the world today through the ministry of Rick Warren and others who are descendants of the blessings of prayers prayed years before their birth.

How far-reaching are your prayers? Consider the impact your prayers can have on the lives of your children and grandchildren. I've experienced this sort of impact directly. I am descended from a long line of believers on my father's side of the family. While I didn't have a great-grandfather who graduated from Spurgeon's Pastor's College, I did have grandparents who prayed. My grandmother, Millie, was one of those prayer warriors. A simple farm girl from Iowa, she and my grandfather raised a family of 11 during the Depression and World War II era. Life was hard, but she had great faith. And she prayed. From her 11 children, only one or two strayed away from the faith. The majority of her grandchildren are believers, and several are involved in ministry.

What do you want your heritage to be? As we pray for our young kids, we usually don't think to pray for their children. But we need to. We need to pray for our children and our children's children, to pray that God would use them in mighty ways—that He would raise up a spiritual army from our family.

SPANNING TIME AND SPACE

Consider the sphere of influence that you have through your prayers. I've seen prayer not only resonate through time but also span continents. We are waging war with principalities and powers—not just in our geographic area, but in other nations as well. Through the power of God and prayer, you can mount an offensive against strongholds all over the world. Imagine the impact you can have beyond your home town. I challenge you: Set your sights beyond your own area, your own family, your own nation.

In my current prayer list, I pray for pastors, missionaries, and friends on every continent (including Antarctica, at times). I have intimate knowledge of the needs in many nations because I am connected with the saints of God there. When you have a vested interest in the lives of others around the world, you gain an interest in the unique needs and challenges that they have. You begin to understand the spiritual warfare that they face, and this better equips you to pray for others as God brings them onto your prayer lists. As time goes on, you begin to not just sympathize but *empathize* with these precious people. And your prayers begin to take shape, passionately aimed at the heart of their needs. Then, spiritual strongholds begin to fall.

THE DEVELOPMENT OF AN OFFENSIVE MINDSET

When your motivation in prayer comes from love and empathy, you will naturally become more intentional. Your warfare against the strongholds of the enemy in prayer will not be defensive, but it will shift to outright campaigns against darkness that you will be leading. You will no longer respond to attacks, but you will mount up on the offensive. You will press against everything that is not of God, and you will experience victory in battle like you've never seen.

God sent Joshua on the offensive to take the promised land. He promised that the land would be taken. He promised that He would be with him. More than once, though, the Lord had to encourage Joshua. Why? Because he was human. Like you and me, he suffered from uncertainty. He battled with unbelief. The words that God spoke to him, the promises He gave to Joshua, resonate in my mind:

> No one will be able to stand against you all the days of your life. As I was with Moses, so I will be with you; I will never leave you nor forsake you. Be strong and courageous, because you will lead these people to inherit the land I swore to their ancestors to give them.
>
> Be strong and very courageous. Be careful to obey all the law which my servant Moses gave you; do not turn from it to the right or to the left, that you may be successful wherever you go. Keep this Book of the Law always on your lips; meditate on it day and night, so that you may be careful to do everything written in it. Then you will be prosperous and successful. Have I not commanded you? Be strong and courageous. Do not be afraid; do not be discouraged, for the LORD your God will be with you wherever you go (Josh 1:5-9).

If God is for us, who can be against us? (This is a rhetorical question—you already know the answer.) As the Lord was with Joshua, He will be with you and me.

When we resolve to heed His Word, He will resolve to prosper our prayers wherever we go. We can pray for India, and God will prosper our prayers. We can pray for China, and God will prosper our prayers. We are commanded by God to pray, and we can take encouragement from God's living, powerful Word. Listen to these words as though your Father in heaven were speaking them directly to you. Hear what He says, and go on the offensive. "Have I not commanded you? Be strong and courageous. Do not be afraid; do not be discouraged, for the LORD your God will be with you wherever you go" (Josh 1:9).

2009
NATIONAL PRAYER
BETH MOORE

Father in heaven,

We lift our eyes toward Your throne, where You reign in righteousness.

Your Word assures us that when Your people cry out in sincerity and humility, You will never turn a deaf ear to us.

We call upon You now, seeking Your forgiveness and favor.

Look over this fevered landscape and heal us, Lord.

Drop knees to the floor and raise eyes to the sky, for we know where our help comes from.

Unite these states again in devotion to You, and blur every dividing line.

Do not give us over to our sins. Give us, instead, over to passionate prayer that moves Your heart.

"May your unfailing love be with us, LORD, even as we put our hope in you."[1]

In the name of our Lord and Savior,

Amen.

CHAPTER 9

STRATEGIC PLANNING: APPROACHING PRAYER INTENTIONALLY

DION ELMORE

Every branch of the military has a basic training program to equip their recruits with the skill sets that they will need in order to carry out their objectives in warfare. They are issued a field manual, an exhaustive volume created for the purpose of training in the finer points of strategy and activity in war.

I came across a copy of the *Army Field Manual* a while back and noticed many parallels between their physical warfare and our spiritual warfare. Learning how to evaluate targets, develop a strategy for attack, and assess damage done are essential whether you're waging war in the physical or spiritual realm. Every soldier in service for their country must learn to wage war.

When I compare Christians to earthly soldiers, I see most engaged in worldly pursuits, like a reservist. Those involved in the reserves aren't full-time soldiers, they're citizen soldiers—an army in reserve, ready at any time to be called up when needed. Whether full time or reserve, the requirements for training are the same: Every soldier must go through basic training, and every soldier must have continual training along the way to remain sharp and skilled.

As a church, our basic training occurs on the job. Most are citizen soldiers who have a responsibility to work by day and fight by night. For a period of time, we must lay down our earthly pursuits and train for battle. We must keep our field manual close at hand. We must work hard to gain the training and knowledge we'll need to be effective.

KNOW YOUR ENEMY

During our training, we will learn the tactics that we will need to win. We will intimately learn the wiles and weapons of our enemy. I remember my father telling me that in basic training for the Navy in World War II, he had to memorize the shapes and sounds of enemy aircraft. They had to be able to identify an aircraft by their silhouettes and decibels so that the enemy would not be able to sneak up on them. In the 1986 Clint Eastwood movie, *Heartbreak Ridge,* seasoned gunnery sergeant Tom "Gunny" Highway is training his recruits when he stops, pulls out an automatic rifle, and begins to shoot live ammunition over their heads. His recruits dive to the ground, and Gunny Highway speaks these memorable words: "This is the AK-47 assault rifle, the preferred weapon of your enemy. It makes a distinctive sound when fired at you. So remember it." In order to be acquainted with your enemy's weapons, you must be exposed to them.

Knowing the tactics and the patterns that the enemy of our soul uses will be essential in recognizing an attack when it occurs. The patterns of our flesh are consistent, and they are similar to those of our fathers and our fathers' fathers. And the devil generally isn't original in his tactics. If your grandfather struggled with pride, your father struggled with pride, and you're struggling with pride, guess what tactic the enemy will use on you? Guard against your weakest area because you will be attacked at your weakest point. Recognize your weaknesses, your vulnerabilities—the parts of you that are "open to assault."

VULNERABILITY ASSESSMENT

How vulnerable are you? Have you put on the "whole armor of God"? Are you practicing using your weapons? Are you skilled in defending yourself against the "fiery darts" that are continually being launched in your direction?

Most losses in battle occur—and most setbacks in ministry happen—because we have not been more thorough in our self-examination. Along with our own examination, with the psalmist in Psalm 26:2, we cry out to the Lord, "Test me, LORD, and try me, examine my heart and my mind." The purpose is to reveal any "wicked way" or weakness that may be in us. When we cry out, the Lord reveals our vulnerable places. We can then deal with them and strengthen any area that is weak.

Why is this important? Because the enemy will attack us in your area of greatest weakness. As we seek the Lord's examination in prayer, He will not only expose the area of greatest weakness in our life, but He will also expose the weaknesses in the lives of those we're praying for. As the Lord exposes areas of weakness, we should begin to pray specifically for those areas, carefully focusing our prayers.

Overestimating the strength of our opposition can be equally destructive. We know from God's Word that any of *their* weapons are ultimately ineffective against those who are in Christ. When we take action in prayer, we must understand that "'no weapon formed against you shall prosper, and every tongue which rises against you in judgment you shall condemn. This is the heritage of the servants of the LORD, and their righteousness is from Me" (Isa 54:17 NKJV). Psalm 27:1 proclaims that "the LORD is my light and my salvation; whom shall I fear? The LORD is the strength of my life; of whom shall I be afraid?" (NKJV). Romans 8:31 asks us a rhetorical question: "What then shall we say to these things? If God is for us, who can be against us?" (NKJV). Not angels, nor principalities, nor powers. Those are great odds!

TARGETING

In the *Army Field Manual*, the objective of targeting is determining "what to attack, how to acquire those targets, and when those targets are acquired, how to attack them in a way that disrupts, delays or limits the enemy's ability to achieve his objectives."[1] How would you like to be so focused in your prayers that you know just what to pray for, what to pray against, and how to "disrupt, delay or limit the enemy's ability to achieve his objectives"? You *can* be that focused. By choosing a few key areas to focus your attention on, you can sharply increase your effectiveness in prayer.

To effectively target needs, challenges, and strongholds with our prayers, we must know what we're aiming at. If we fail to aim, we will fail to hit our target every time. So what should our prayer targets be? What should make up the content and direction of our prayers? Over the last several years, I've identified a simple strategy to help me keep my prayers on target. I also use the same pattern to teach others how to effectively target their prayers.

The first troops to be sent into any conflict are the scouts. Their job is reconnaissance: the exploration conducted to gain information. One of the greatest reconnaissance tools in your arsenal are your ears. People will reveal to you in conversation the strongholds that they are fighting against. You simply have to listen. I want to encourage you to buy a small notebook and make a habit of carrying that and a pen or pencil with you at all times. Begin to strike up conversations with people, take out your pad and pen, and ask them if you might make a few notes because you'd like to pray for them. You will be amazed how they will open up simply because they know that you are sincerely interested in their needs.

While many prayer needs will be specific to that person and their situation, I've found that you can ask some very simple probing questions that will help you identify their prayer needs. Have you ever heard of the Pareto principle? You may know it better as the 80/20 rule. It states that for many events in life, 80 percent of the effects come from 20 percent of the causes. In other words, if you can identify and address the 20 percent of the causes, 80 percent of the effects or issues will disappear.

Over the last 20 years of ministry, I've been able to identify several key life issues that seem to generate about 80 percent of people's life struggles:

- Life purpose
- Communication
- Relationship
- Marriage
- Parenting
- Finances
- Sexuality

The list isn't exhaustive by any means, but it is a good guideline for gauging how and where people are struggling. The best way to help others deal with these strongholds is to listen and ask questions. As you show sincere interest in people's lives and let them know that you are going to be praying for them, you'll be amazed at their responsiveness.

Imagine this scenario: One of your coworkers is struggling with her marriage, and the key issues are communication and finances. If you ask if you can pray for her, 9 out of 10 times she'll say, "Sure." As you begin to pray, make a point to check in and ask how things are progressing. As you focus on praying for these areas, you can also encourage her with tools to help her understand how to get these areas under control. You will see great victories in her life.

You can begin to pray for whole communities this way—that people would find hope and purpose, that they would be freed from the bondage of debt and from sexual immorality. If 80 percent of people struggle with these issues, imagine how much good targeting these areas would do in freeing many in our communities from bondage.

Another place to target strongholds is in our communities. To do this, we must become students of the news. When we watch our local news or read our local paper, what do we see? I look for patterns and areas that are consistently in the news. I know which parts of town have the highest instances of drugs, crime, gang activity, and prostitution. I can also tell you which areas of our community have the most affluence and influence. I pay attention to prevalent issues in individual school districts. I know the civic leaders by name, the heads of the school districts, the community influencers and power brokers. I pay attention to the economy and its effects on the individual neighborhoods—which schools are closing, how many families are affected, which neighborhoods have the most for-sale signs. If we pay attention, we will always have areas, issues, and people to specifically target with our prayers.

Alongside these more common issues, there seems to be an almost endless list of other areas of bondage that exist in people's lives. Over the last 10 years, I've seen a marked increase in the struggles that people experience. The most common concerns I've encountered are mental and emotional issues like depression, bipolar disorder, and panic and anxiety disorders, as well as the mental and emotional effects of the drugs associated with their treatment. Areas of sexual sin like fornication, adultery, and pornography are very common strongholds, with substance addictions to alcohol and illegal and prescription drugs following close behind.

As you become more familiar with the needs and strongholds in your area, ask the Lord to reveal His heart and desires to you through prayer. Every area of ungodliness in our personal lives and in our communities grieves the heart of God. His will is that all evil is rooted out and that His light and righteousness rule and reign. Begin holding a regular prayer meeting where everyone who has a burden to pray can attend. Together in one accord, you can pray and seek direction as to which strongholds He would have you attack together.

PREPARING YOUR PLAN TO PRAY

An old saying goes, "If you fail to plan, you plan to fail." Prayer is no different. In order to experience consistent victory in intercessory prayer, we must make ourselves a prayer plan— a scheme or method of doing. We must prepare in advance and be organized. In our plan, we should include prayers for our leaders, churches, country, community, work, school, families, friends, neighbors, coworkers, and whomever else the Lord brings to our minds.

Step 1: Develop a prayer plan.

Most Christians are free-form in their prayer life. They pray general prayers at general times and in general places. They don't want to be constrained by a plan; they want to go with the flow as the Holy Spirit reveals what they are to pray for.

This sounds very spiritual on the surface, but when you walk with true prayer warriors, you find that there is always a method to their praying. You also find that they are very disciplined in carrying out their plan. To have a developed a strategic plan doesn't take away from the Spirit's leading; rather, it enhances it. You can be led by the Spirit and stay on task; it's not an either/or choice, but a both/and approach.

When we are praying specifically, we are continually bringing to mind, adding to, and subtracting from the prayer needs that are in front of us. Much like memorization of Scripture, continued repetition of prayer helps keep the most important things at the forefront of our minds. The things we think about become the things that we focus on. Inspiration is the first part, and then comes the tough part: acting on what we know.

Step 2: Work the plan.

Most people who are determined prayer warriors find that prayer is a true discipline and labor when pursued with passion. The difficulty for us comes in the form of being faithful to pray. Effective, fervent prayer—specific and directed prayer—is not easy. When we engage in intercessory prayer for others, we move ahead with the understanding that there are specific targets to hit and that keeping the pressure on those targets will take time.

The Roman armies had a long-term strategy for tearing down strongholds. They would scout around a walled fortress and look for its weaknesses. Then, they would bring in supplies and establish a camp around the stronghold. After this, they would lay siege to it while simultaneously building towers and ramps. They used this strategy when they attacked Jerusalem in AD 70. According to Josephus, a Jewish historian who observed this attack from the Roman side as a prisoner, the siege was successful, but only after five months of severe fighting.

The harder we pray, the harder the battle will be. The devil and his demons don't like having their encampments routed by prayer, and they will most certainly retaliate. As the counterattacks come, we must respond with greater intensity and effort to keep the offensive going. We must keep up the attack and use every weapon at our disposal. There will be seasons when you see victory, and there will be seasons when you feel as though the victory belongs to the enemy. It's all about perseverance and faithfulness. Your charge is to pray.

Step 3: Develop a regular prayer list.

Once we've developed our prayer plan, assessed the needs, identified strongholds, and realized that this is a long-term commitment to be faithful, we must create our list. Keeping lists of prayer needs is a simple way to stay on target and measure progress; keep track of who, what, and when, and then add what happened. I'd suggest always having your Bible, a notebook to write your lists on, and a pencil or pen when you pray.

Record notes on your list. If you take notes from your scouting exercises and any letters or newsletters you get from your missionary friends, you will end up with a scrapbook of notes about your community needs. Then begin to pray. Pray as the Holy Spirit leads. He will give you supernatural insight into other things you've not written down; when He does, write those things down and add them to your list. Remember, prayer is dynamic, and it is always changing. You should always be ready to modify your prayer list. As your list begins to grow, you will need to set aside dedicated time to pray each day. Get into the habit and develop the discipline.

Step 4: Take time to pray.

Time is a precious commodity. We speak in concepts of "spending" or "saving" when we talk about it. Like money, we never seem to have enough—we always wish we had more. Everyone has the same amount given to them each week, but some people accomplish so much with theirs, and others accomplish very little.

Priorities dictate how we choose to spend our time. We live out what we value, and our lives speak volumes about what is truly important to us. As Christians, we know that the Word of God is critical to our health and well-being, and we know that we must have strong relationships with other believers. We also know that prayer is the key to having a vibrant relationship with Jesus and having a powerful ministry toward others. If these things are all true, why is it so difficult to give our time to these things?

It really boils down to two things: misplaced priorities and a lack of discipline. For most of us, "discipline" is not a pleasant word; when we hear it, we think of punishment. But instead, we should be thinking of faithfulness. We all live in a busy culture, and we lead very busy lives; in fact, busyness is probably one of the greatest enemies of prayer. For many of us, prayer may mean that we have to get up earlier or stay up later to get time alone with God. Unfortunately, this usually works to our disadvantage, and we become tired. If we're tired, prayer becomes increasingly difficult.

The best way to work around tiredness is to plan your prayer times for some time during the day when you're wide awake. As you make time in your schedule and prioritize your time to pray, you will by necessity eliminate many of the things that are presently consuming you. Are you a morning person or a night owl? When do you have the most energy? What times do you usually choose to do the things that you like most? We often choose to do things we love during our most energetic times. Who would go to a movie at the end of the day when they're fatigued? They might fall asleep. Unfortunately, that is exactly when most of us remember to pray, and we end up offering snoring instead of supplication. Give God the best time of your day. Pray with your spouse or friends. Choose an evening during the week and gather together.

And remember this: We don't really have much time. The days are growing more and more evil, life is becoming more dangerous and difficult, and we're not getting any younger. I periodically stroll through a local cemetery to regain perspective. I typically choose the older graves because many of them list more information about the individuals and families buried there. These people all lived their lives like we do. They were beloved fathers, mothers, sisters, brothers, sons, and daughters. They had loves and dreams, work and troubles, just like you and me. And the only thing left of them is an old stone with a few words. This is how it will be for us all. James made a powerful statement: "For what is your life? It is even a vapor that appears for a little time and then vanishes away" (Jas 4:14 NKJV). Don't let your life vanish away without accomplishing what God has placed you here on the earth to do. Choose to pray, and He will bless your investment.

Step 5: Journal answers to prayer.

A soldier wouldn't be worth his weight if he didn't keep track of his victories. No soldier would report back to his commanding officer and say, "I'm not sure what I hit, but I think I hit something." In warfare and prayer, we need to track our victories. As you pray, pay attention to how the Lord begins to answer, and record what you observe in your prayer journal.

Keeping track of God's answers brings encouragement. The Lord had the children of Israel erect stone monuments to remind them of what He had accomplished in their midst. The people in the nations surrounding the Israelites may not have observed the parting of the Red Sea, but they did hear about it; and when they did, the result was a fear of the God of Israel. When we recognize how God has answered prayer, we remain encouraged, people hear and realize who our God is, and we continue to pray.

As we journal, we must always remember that prayer takes time. If we are praying against strongholds that the enemy has controlled for a long time, it may take a while to pull them down. I've been praying for some people for over 20 years. In some cases, I'm still waiting to see God move, but I haven't seen any change. The issue for me is not just seeing the change, but my dedication to these people over time. Even though it's been years, my passion for them and for their salvation and freedom has only grown.

The more we acknowledge what the Lord has done, the more we see the impact that we have had. Remember, it is about your discipline and desire to tarry with the Lord. Leave the results up to God to answer in His timing, which may not be in your lifetime.

UNLIMITED

Andrew Murray exhorted us, "Beware in your prayers, above everything else, of limiting God, not only by unbelief, but by fancying that you know what He can do. Expect unexpected things 'above all that we ask or think.' "[2]

When we pray but don't see immediate answers, it's easy for unbelief to enter and for the devil to challenge our faith. If he can convince us not to expect great things, he can get us to question our effectiveness and even God's ability. Ephesians 3:20–21 offers us assurance: "Now to Him who is able to do exceedingly abundantly above all that we ask or think, according to the power that works in us, to Him be glory in the church by Christ Jesus to all generations, forever and ever" (NKJV).

What can you ask of God that He cannot accomplish? What plan can you conceive that is beyond His ability to perform? When you doubt, remember that our God is able. When you don't see His hand moving, remember that *He is able*. He can accomplish anything, and nothing is beyond His power.

If God is for us and He is able, what do we have to lose? If we can train in prayer to tear down strongholds in people's lives and have an impact, why wouldn't we? If we know that life is short and that we're not guaranteed tomorrow, why wouldn't we spend our time making a difference in people's lives throughout the world? If we really believe these things, we will rise up in prayer.

The goal is to finish the race well, to get to end of our lives, face Jesus, and hear Him say, "Well done! You did all that you could do! You 'fought the good fight!' You prevailed in prayer! You made an impact! Well done!"

NATIONAL PRAYER

FRANKLIN GRAHAM

Lord,

We are thankful for the abundant blessings You have bestowed on America. Our forefathers looked to You as protector, provider, and the promise of hope. But we have wandered far from that firm foundation. May we repent for turning our backs on Your faithfulness.

We pray that this great nation will be restored by Your forgiveness.

From bondage, You grant freedom.

Through Your own sacrifice, You offer salvation.

From the state of despair, You offer peace.

From the bounties of heaven, You have blessed—not because of our goodness—but by Your grace.

You have given us freedom to worship You in spirit and in truth as Your holy Word instructs. May our lives honor You in word and deed. May our nation acknowledge that all good things come from the Father above.

President Abraham Lincoln proclaimed that our nation should set apart a day for national prayer to confess our sins and transgressions in sorrow, "yet with assured hope that genuine repentance will lead to mercy and pardon... announced in the Holy Scriptures and proven by all history, that those nations only are blessed whose God is the Lord." He continues:

> We have vainly imagined, in the deceitfulness of our hearts, that all these blessings were produced by some superior wisdom and virtue of our own ... we have become

too self-sufficient to feel the necessity of redeeming and preserving grace, too proud to pray to the God that made us. It behooves us, then, ... to confess our national sins, and to pray for clemency and forgiveness.[1]

Help us to pray earnestly for our president and leaders who govern, that they will humble themselves and seek Your guidance so that everything we do will shine the light of Your glory in a darkened world.

May our prayers as a people and a nation be heard and blessed for such a time as this. We make this plea in faith, believing in the mighty name of Jesus our Lord.

Amen.

CHAPTER 10

PREPARING FOR BATTLE

JOHN BORNSCHEIN

H ave you ever read about the mighty men of King David (1 Chr 12:8–14)? These men were of great valor and physical strength. The Knights of the Round Table had nothing on them. First Chronicles 12:22 describes, "For day by day men came to David to help him, until there was a great army like the army of God" (NASB). Jashobeam killed 300 men with his spear in one battle (1 Chr 11:11–25), and Abishai struck down hundreds as well (2 Sam 23:18).

My favorite of these mighty men is Eleazar (2 Sam 23:9–10). While the armies fled from the Philistines, he stood his ground and brought down so many men that his hand froze to the sword. Eleazar had such courage that the armies of Israel were rallied and returned to defeat the enemy. Talk about faith and courage under fire! The enemy was strong. They were outnumbered and being defeated, but it took just one to stand firm and hold the line. He didn't do it alone; God was with him. But Eleazar had to be willing to allow God to work through him, to serve as an instrument or an extension of God's own hand. Eleazar had to take that first step, and the Almighty empowered him to do the rest.

I trained in the martial arts for years. Recently, I became a student in the combat style known as jujitsu. When competing with weapons, we would engage in a tournament known as "king of the hill." The objective was to own the ring by battling each person who entered one at a time until you yourself were defeated. This would often occur after the "king" was utterly exhausted. The interesting thing is that no matter how well you conditioned, this would not take very long.

I remember defeating three well-rested men in the ring. I took a beating, but I was respected for standing my ground against three trained combatants. When I read the verses of the mighty men of David for the first time, I was literally in awe. It seemed unfathomable that a man could physically overcome 300 men. These weren't just farmers either—we're talking 300 *warriors*. Only God could grant that kind of physical strength to any human being. (This was not uncommon; Samson was granted that power as well.)

War is waged in several forms. God would often send Israel into battle, frequently executing His judgment where required. Since Adam, there may have been more than 14,000 recorded wars and 14 billion deaths.[1] On the other hand, the spiritual battle began well before Adam was even given breath.

A WORLD IN WAR

Revelation declares, "Woe to the earth and the sea, because the devil has come down to you, having great wrath, knowing that he has only a short time" (Rev 12:12 NASB). In this "short time," there will always be war (Ezek 7:25). There is only one peace and only one hope—Jesus Christ, our Lord and King. As Ephesians 2:14 states, "For He Himself is our peace, who made both groups into one, and broke down the barrier of the dividing wall" (NASB).

If you are in Christ, you are a new creation—a child of the King. But being a Christian, a follower of Christ, does not guarantee you peace on earth; you are also an enemy of the one who roams this world. As Jesus said in Matthew 10:34, "Do not think that I came to bring peace on the earth; I did not come to bring peace, but a sword" (NASB). Trouble and trials will come because our hope in Christ is for salvation and a renewed life in the new kingdom (Heb 13:14). Only there—in the new kingdom—will be our true peace. For now, we are tested and tried to be made unto His likeness. Thus, we must prepare for battle—it will come whether we are ready or not. This battle requires training in the physical and the spiritual. Through our struggle, our combat, we are shaped and conformed like iron sharpening iron. In this, the faithful will emerge.

We must put on the armor that our general has given to us and train as diligent soldiers. The first step is to pray—to be on our knees before the King. When a soldier is in prayer, this is sacred and holy ground (Exod 3:5), for where God is, the enemy cannot be. Soldiers must read the Scripture as though they were training with a sword. A knight couldn't pick up a sword at birth and overcome an adversary; likewise, a Christian who is unskilled with the Word of God could not defeat an enemy or save a life.

David did not go to battle without first petitioning the Lord—asking Him for permission to engage and for favor in battle and victory (1 Sam 30:1-19). But how often do we rush to start our day without first going to God in prayer? How often do we lay out our plans and then seek God's counsel and wisdom? Prayer should be our first engagement, not our last response.

KNOWING THE ENEMY

In his first letter to the people of Corinth, Paul writes,

> Do you not know that in a race all the runners run, but only one gets the prize? Run in such a way as to get the prize. Everyone who competes in the games goes into strict training. They do it to get a crown that will not last, but we do it to get a crown that will last forever.

Therefore I do not run like someone running aimlessly; I do not fight like a boxer beating the air. No, I strike a blow to my body and make it my slave so that after I have preached to others, I myself will not be disqualified for the prize (1 Cor 9:24–27).

When I first read these words, I was challenged to understand the context in which Paul was speaking. You see, the boxers he was referring to used gloves made of metal and leather straps rather than the boxing gloves we are familiar with today. Thus when he says that he "strikes" his body, this is not something to take lightly. He was faced with the same temptations we struggle with today. His response was not to shun the enemy but to recognize his own weakness and respond with training and determination. We should apply this diligently in our lives as well. A strong, properly focused will coupled with the Holy Spirit is a powerful combination.

When you are doing God's will, you can expect opposition. When David was called to be the next king of Israel, he was pursued by Saul, and many people wanted to kill him. When Nehemiah was called to rebuild the walls of Jerusalem, he faced many challenges as well. As any warrior knows, it's vital to know who your enemy is so you can understand how to defeat him. Peter offers us this warning about our enemy: "Be alert and of sober mind. Your enemy the devil prowls around like a roaring lion looking for someone to devour" (1 Pet 5:8–9).

Our enemy takes his battle very seriously, and he is out to destroy us and take our crowns. Here are some other characteristics of our adversary:

- He is subtle and wily.
- The devil is spiritual. (Not everything spiritual is righteous.)
- If you are marked by God, the devil has no power over you. You are impervious to death until your mission is complete.

- He can only inflict permissible wounds.
- His primary weapons are deceit and temptation.

ALL OR NOTHING

Psalm 116:15 states, "Precious in the sight of the LORD is the death of his faithful servants." Why? Death is only a passage from one life to the next; the deceased saints gave their lives because they were dedicated to a greater purpose. In *Mere Christianity*, C. S. Lewis writes, "If you read history you will find that the Christians who did most for the present world were just those who thought most of the next. ... It is since Christians have largely ceased to think of the other world that they have become so ineffective in this."[2] The sacrifice of the temporal for the eternal is what separates the wheat from the chaff (Matt 3). There is no room for lukewarm believers in God's kingdom. As Revelation 3:16 states, "Because you are lukewarm, and neither hot nor cold, I will spit you out of My mouth" (NASB).

God doesn't want our sloppy seconds; it is all or nothing. In his book, *Crazy Love*, Francis Chan illustrates what this means:

> When I was in high school, I seriously considered joining the Marines; this was when they first came out with the commercials for "the few, the proud, the Marines." But you know what? I didn't bother to ask if they would modify the rules for me so I could run less, and maybe also do fewer push-ups. That would've been pointless and stupid, and I knew it. Everyone knows that if you sign up for the Marines, you have to do whatever they tell you. They own you. Somehow this realization does not cross over to our thinking about the Christian life. Jesus didn't say that if you wanted to follow Him you could do it in a lukewarm manner. He said, "Take up your cross and follow me."[3]

Either you're a warrior for the Lord or you're not. Make the commitment right now that you are going to lay down your life for the Lord, taking up the cross and following Him.

Christ was confronted with people who were too comfortable with their lives, and He challenged them. He told a son to leave his family and follow Him (Matt 8:21-22). He told a wealthy man that to follow Him would mean total sacrifice, stressing that even the Son of Man didn't have a pillow to lay His head upon (Matt 8:18-20). He told another that he should sell all that he had and give to the poor (Matt 19:16-30). In each case, these eager men were cut to their heart because they wanted to be good but not great. They weren't willing to go all the way. But Jesus promises a reward for full commitment: "And everyone who has left houses or brothers or sisters or father or mother or wife or children or fields for my sake will receive a hundred times as much and will inherit eternal life" (Matt 19:29-30).

When the heat turns up in this society—and it most certainly will—are you going to be willing to walk into the furnace or step into the lion's den for your faith? Will you be willing to give it all for Him? The Holy Spirit will give you strength when that moment comes (Acts 7:54-60), but *you* must take the first step. Ultimately, you will have to count the cost of discipleship. Luke 9:23 tells us that whoever is willing to follow Him must take up their cross and, according to Luke 14:25-35, be willing to give it all for the cause of Christ. We are warned that if we turn back, we are unfit for the kingdom (Luke 9:62).

In 1 Kings 19:19-21, we are told of Elisha and the events that occurred when he was called. Elijah comes to town, puts the mantle on Elisha and tells him, "Let's go." The call was instant. Elisha had to make a decision. So, he took his plow, burned it, and sacrificed his cattle. This would be the equivalent of selling your business to go into full-time ministry. There was no "plan B" for Elisha. It was all or nothing.

Rarely is God's calling on our life convenient. He intentionally forces us out of our comfort zones to engage in ministry. Keep alert, listen, and be ready. Your calling may be right now.

FACING A DEFEATED ENEMY

Adrian Rogers said, "Satan's real war is not with you ... it is with God. Evil persons have always known that if they cannot harm someone directly, harm someone that they love and you've hurt them. Satan's war is with God, but he has set his attack on you because God has set His affection on you."[4] Satan wants you in a constant state of turmoil, a constant state of fear. He wants you to focus on your growing time constraints, the pending layoff or financial pressures, illnesses, and other distractions because he wants you to begin to doubt God's provision, God's promises, and God's love for you.

Paul tells us how we may live victoriously in this present evil age in spite of satanic opposition: We live victoriously through God's ability and the power of His might. In John 17:15, Jesus prayed to the Father, "My prayer is not that you take them out of the world but that you protect them from the evil one." It's important that we don't underestimate Satan, but it's just as important that we don't *overestimate* his power either. You and I face a defeated enemy. Jesus paid the price; He destroyed and annihilated the works of the devil. Now you can face all your battles with the armies of heaven at your side. It's like a mopping up operation in which the war has already been won and there remain only a few battles.

What feeds the Spirit is that which drives the mind and directs the body. Read this verse: "And now, compelled by the Spirit, I am going to Jerusalem, not knowing what will happen to me there. I only know that in every city the Holy Spirit warns me that prison and hardships are facing me. However, I consider my life worth nothing to me; my only aim is to finish the race and complete the task the Lord Jesus has given me—the task of testifying to the good news of God's grace" (Acts 20:22-24). Paul was so dedicated to kingdom work that he was no longer deterred by physical abuse. He was on a mission.

In the book of Acts, Paul knows the enemy lies ahead and will surely harm him for speaking truth. But does he turn back and run? No. He perseveres, knowing that cuts, bruises, and broken bones are no obstacle for truth. And he counts these hardships all joy, for the greater good of the ministry to which he was called. That is passion—taking up a cross and modeling the One who gave it all.

> "Lord, even the demons are subject to us in Your name." And He said to them, "I saw Satan fall like lightning from heaven. Behold, I give you the authority to trample on serpents and scorpions, and over all the power of the enemy, and nothing shall by any means hurt you. Nevertheless do not rejoice in this, that the spirits are subject to you, but rather rejoice because your names are written in heaven."
>
> (Luke 10:17-20 NKJV)

Almighty God,

You are our mighty fortress, our refuge and the God in whom we place our trust. As our nation faces great distress and uncertainty, we ask Your Holy Spirit to fall afresh upon Your people—convict us of sin and inflame within us a passion to pray for our land and its people. We long for peace and justice within our borders, and so we lift before You our leaders in government, our families, our communities, and those in law enforcement and the armed services. Grant each an awareness of their desperate need of wisdom and salvation in You, until sin becomes a reproach to all and true righteousness exalts this nation.

Protect and defend us against our enemies, and may the cause of Christ always prevail against those who seek our harm. Raise Yourself up in the midst of our schools, courts and homes, and most of all, Your church. You are mighty to save, so please send a spirit of revival and renewal, and may it begin in our own hearts.

Remember America, we pray. Remember the foundations on which this country was built. Remember the prayers of our nation's fathers and mothers, and do not forget us in our time of need. We confess our sin, praise Your name, laud Your gospel, and commit to extending Your grace to all, especially the poor and needy. Thank You for listening to our cry, for You are greatly to be praised!

In the name of our Savior, Jesus Christ,

Amen.

CHAPTER 11

THE WHOLE ARMOR OF GOD

JOHN BORNSCHEIN AND BRIAN TOON

Every day, as we pull out of the driveway, my family puts on armor, piece by piece. One of us will lead, saying, "And we put of the helmet of ... salvation!" It isn't just any armor that we put on, it's the armor of God that Paul instructs his readers to put on in Ephesians:

> Take up the full armor of God, so that you may be able to resist in the evil day, and having done everything, to stand firm. Stand firm therefore, having *girded your loins with truth*, and having put on the *breastplate of righteousness*, and having shod your *feet* with the *preparation of the gospel of peace*; in addition to all, taking up the *shield of faith* with which you will be able to extinguish all the flaming missiles of the evil *one*. And take *the helmet of salvation*, and the *sword of the Spirit*, which is the *word of God*. With all prayer and petition *pray* at all times in the Spirit, and with this in view, be

on the alert with all perseverance and petition for all
the saints (Eph 6:13–18 NASB, emphasis added).

Verbalizing each step is a great way to remind us of God's promise of our protection. God didn't just provide us with armor, He
gave us *His* armor. Certainly God's armor is more than sufficient
if we will just wear it and let it work—every day. But we need
the *whole* armor; missing just one piece leaves us vulnerable.

THE BELT OF TRUTH

In the New Testament era, men wore robes or gowns. When
they fought or ran, they had to tuck their robes into their gir-
dles, what we would call a belt. The belt of truth allows us to
fight without being entangled in our garments. Those who do
not surround themselves with truth will become entangled in
their own web of deceit and will fall.

Centuries ago, men would wrestle with only a belt because it
was the first and preparatory piece of armor that a soldier wore.
The object of the match was to remove the opponent's belt. If Satan
can disarm us of our belt of truth, he can defeat us; deceit and
lies are his greatest weapons. If we are under his control, it is
because we have believed one of his lies instead of the truth of
God's Word. Jesus said, "I am ... the truth" (John 14:6). To wear
the belt of truth is to look toward Jesus to lead the way, to have
your eyes singled only on Him.

THE BREASTPLATE OF RIGHTEOUSNESS

The word "righteousness" means a "pure life." Satan attacks
with impurity, trying to break through the plates of the armor.
We need to be aware of sin and to deal with it ruthlessly when
it first presents itself, before it fully penetrates our breastplate.

Scripture mentions two basic kinds of righteousness. First
is man's righteousness, which is the righteousness that people
attempt to accomplish and perform without Christ. Isaiah tells
us that "all our righteous acts are like filthy rags" (Isa 64:6). This

self-righteousness has no value to God. The second type of righteousness is God's own righteousness, which is imputed to us at salvation. God's righteousness comes only through faith; it is a gift and appropriated through Christ. Righteousness gives us total acceptance with God through Jesus.

Isaiah 59:17 specifically mentions the Messiah wearing the helmet of salvation and the breastplate of righteousness. With that breastplate, Jesus faced every temptation of Satan with 100 percent victory. He was 100 percent obedient to the Father, and He was "without blemish and without spot" (1 Pet 1:19 NKJV). Now, God has given us that same breastplate to us so that we, too, can live a holy and undefiled life. The moment you received Christ by faith, you were cleansed of all sin and clothed in Christ's breastplate of righteousness. Through Christ, you have power over sin; you are no longer controlled by your sinful nature but by His Spirit within you. That breastplate stands against lust, greed, envy, and jealousy. But we must be steadfast to resist temptation.

We often think that the outward expression of anger will put a person in their place. But "the wrath of man does not produce the righteousness of God" (Jas 1:20 NKJV). Anger against another person makes us play right into the hand of the devil. The way to overcome the spiritual powers that come against us through individuals is to turn the other cheek (Matt 5:39) and take the issue up in prayer.

FEET SHOD WITH THE GOSPEL OF PEACE

The military shoes (which are similar to football cleats) not only allowed soldiers to move rapidly, but they also gave them stability in hand-to-hand combat. In the spiritual realm, the shoes of the gospel of peace make a messenger prepared to share the glad tidings of peace.

Life often brings obstacles, slippery slopes, and discouragement that attempts to make you lose your footing and stumble. Do you have the peace of God to enable you to walk through any difficulty? For me, whenever discouraging thoughts arise, my peace comes from reminding myself of how God has provided for me in the past while reciting Bible verses that promise prosperity and peace.

THE SHIELD OF FAITH

Faith comes from God, who squelches all of Satan's fiery darts. We need to constantly inspect and reinforce this shield of faith by reminding ourselves of all of the times the Lord has achieved victory. Ephesians 6:16 teaches us that our shield of faith will quench *all* the fiery darts of the wicked. Once a person starts standing on the Word of God, the attack intensifies (2 Tim 3:12; Mark 4:17). But victory over all the attacks of the enemy is possible.

Paul says, "Now thanks be to God who always leads us in triumph in Christ" (2 Cor 2:14 NKJV). Teaching that God wills us to fail at times is like telling an athlete that his coach wants him to lose. We all learn from defeats and experiencing a loss can refine us, but real winners never plan to lose. Christians who plan to lose *will* lose.

THE HELMET OF SALVATION

The helmet is a constant reminder of the deliverance that God gives us; in the end, we have won the war against Satan. What the helmet was to the Roman soldier, salvation is to the Christian soldier. There can be no victory unless the mind is protected with God's Word.

Romans 8:6 says, "For to be carnally minded is death, but to be spiritually minded is life and peace" (NKJV). A significant battlefield for Christians is in the area of our minds. We must be careful to protect ourselves from wrong or improper thought patterns and be transformed by the renewing of our minds (Rom 12:2). Every thought can be brought captive to the obedience of Jesus Christ (2 Cor 10:4–5).

The Roman helmet also protected the jawbone, with armor extending down to the chin. We must control our tongues and speak words that glorify God (Eph 4:29; Jas 3:1–12), stating that we have overcome the darkness and that no weapon formed against us shall prosper.

THE SWORD OF THE SPIRIT

God doesn't mean for us to fight a defensive battle; He doesn't intend for us to just suit up in our armor and take blow after blow from the enemy without striking back. That's why He's given us the sword of His Spirit—His living Word contained in the Bible.

It's not the Bible lying on your coffee table that makes the enemy flee, but the trained mind filled with the knowledge of truth, activated by the power of the Holy Spirit and exercised in an appropriate situation. It's similar to what Jesus said in the Gospel of John: "the words that I speak unto you, they are spirit, and they are life" (John 6:63 KJV).

The sword is only useful if you keep it sharp. Keep your knowledge of God's Word sharp by constantly reading it, meditating on it, and speaking His promises. Satan loves to keep us out of the Word. To make Scripture reading and meditation a priority, we need to think of it as more important than food or sleep. Then it will take on a whole new perspective.

FIGHT THE GOOD FIGHT

In one of his letters, Paul encouraged Timothy to "fight well in the Lord's battles" (1 Tim 1:18 NLT). The incredible thing to remember is that we are not alone in this battle. We need only to ask for the courage and God will be with us. In 2 Kings, when Elisha asked God to "open his eyes that he may see," God "opened the servant's eyes, and he saw; and behold, the mountain was full of horses and chariots of fire all around Elisha" (2 Kgs 6:17 NASB). Just like Elisha, we also can go bearing the seal of the Most High, and we will never, ever be alone.

Judges 6–8 offers the incredible story of Gideon, who God chose to lead a band of only 300 men against thousands. God appointed an unqualified military leader and stripped him of soldiers, thinning out their numbers and selecting only the ones who would give it all for Him. Then He told them to put their weapons away. What kind of general does that? But that is exactly how God works. God didn't reveal His plan until the men had fully committed to go where He led. When God acts, He explodes boundaries and forces us to go where we aren't comfortable, and then He does a work that is awesome and unbelievable. Just as the Father drove the enemy into submission before Gideon, He will break down strongholds through you.

Here are some important points to remember:

- **Armor is essential to our survival as Christian soldiers, but we are not invincible**. We are on our knees always. Only God grants victory, and sometimes He allows injury to stimulate growth for the greater good.

- **We must function as a unit.** If one person is weak and undisciplined, he or she can pull the whole army down. We must take courage and be strong, supporting one another and doing our part to fortify the unit. As Hebrews 10:24–25 states, "Let us consider how to stimulate one another to love and good deeds, not forsaking our own assembling together, as is a habit of some, but encouraging one another" (NASB). There is strength in numbers; we need to value the soldier who is with us.

- **Take the enemy seriously.** We need to take our purpose in life seriously. We are not here to be self-serving. We have a mission, so let's get to it.

When we put on the full armor of God, we are only positioning ourselves for battle; we then need to take the field of battle in prayer. Prayer is not just what we do before the battle; frequently, it is the battle. Prayer is what accomplishes results. This is evident in Exodus 17, when Moses stood on a hill overlooking

Joshua and the Israelite army engaged in battle with the Amalekites. As Moses stood firm, rod in hand, he prayed over the battle. When his arms, raised in prayer, grew weary and fell, the tide turned against Joshua and his army. But when his arms were lifted high, they began to overcome and victory was at hand. The soldiers fought the Amalekites in the valley below, and on the hill above, Moses waged battle in prayer.

When Moses' arms grew tired, he sat on a stone while Aaron and Hur held his hands up—one on each side. In that way, his hands remained steady till sunset, and Joshua was victorious. His prayer won the battle in conjunction with what was done in the natural. Leaders must cover those on the front line in intercession before the Father, and it is critical that we do our part to be available and provide physical aid whenever and wherever it is necessary to do the Lord's work. This mission is a tandem effort as we engage the enemy on all fronts.

Another great example of a battle won by prayer is found in 2 Kings 19: King Hezekiah prayed as the Assyrian army marched toward the city of Jerusalem. God heard the prayers of Hezekiah, and that night, an angel of the Lord struck down 185,000 warriors in the Assyrian camp. We are told that, in the morning, the people of Judah went out and found all the dead bodies (2 Kgs 19:35). They didn't even have to lift their swords. God went before them by the prayer of His faithful servant—and the battle was won.

PRAYER WINS

In Matthew 21:21–22, Jesus encouraged His disciples with these words: "Truly I say to you, if you have faith, and do not doubt, you shall not only do what was done to the fig tree, but even if you say to this mountain, 'Be taken up and cast into the sea,' it shall happen. And all things you ask in prayer, believing, you shall receive" (NASB). Prayer is another form of absolute dependence and reliance upon God for His divine intervention. Remember these points:

- **There is a right way and a wrong way to pray.**
  Fortunately, God is patient and looks to the heart.
  Remember, you are no stronger than your prayer life.

- **Prayer is communion with God**—fellowship, relationship, and intimacy with Him. The devil wants to keep us
  from praying. He mocks our schemes and laughs at our
  toiling, but he also fears our prayers.

- **Asking is *one* aspect of prayer, but it is not *the* purpose of prayer**. The purpose of God granting requests is
  that the Father would be glorified through the name of
  His Son.

- **Prayer is conversation**; it is dialogue, not monologue.
  It's not just petitioning God with two choices: "God, please
  do A or B." We must ask Him for what He wants, too, and
  then be prepared to submit to His will. We need to meditate on His Word, and then "Be still, and know that [He is]
  God" (Psa 46:10).

- **Prayer builds perception.** Are you blessed or stressed?
  When you magnify God, you realize just how insignificant
  your problems really are. Praise Him for the blessings you
  have rather than just bombarding Him with perceptions
  of what you lack. If you are caving into stress, step up
  your prayer life and Scripture reading in proportion to
  the intensity of the attack.

It's easy to get caught up in the delights of this world, but we
need to try hard not to lay up treasures here. When we read
James 4:13–15, which says that we are a vapor, it is easy to realize
our place. Ecclesiastes 5:15 serves as another reminder of this:
"As he [the rich man] had come naked from his mother's womb,
so will he return as he came. He will take nothing from the fruit
of his labor that he can carry in his hand" (NASB). The Father
implores us to avoid the desires of our sin nature: "What good
will it be for someone to gain the whole world, yet forfeit their

soul? Or what can anyone give in exchange for their soul?" (Matt 16:26). We belong to the Lord, and every day is a gift.

As culture continues to crumble by casting out truth for moral relativism (godlessness and lawlessness), we must realize that the church is a stronghold in this world. We are lifting the standard on the battlefield, and we must stand firm. Remember the words of Deuteronomy 20:3-4: "Today you are going into battle against your enemies. Do not be fainthearted or afraid; do not panic or be terrified by them. For the LORD your God is the one who goes with you to fight for you against your enemies to give you victory." We must be confident that the Lord will grant us victory (Prov 21:31).

NATIONAL PRAYER

DAVID JEREMIAH

Heavenly Father,

Every good gift and perfect gift comes from You. You are a faithful God, and Your mercy endures forever.

You have promised to bless the nation that trusts in You. Our currency proclaims "In God We Trust," but in our culture we are far from You.

In the words of the prophet Daniel, "we have sinned and committed iniquity, we have done wickedly and rebelled, even by departing from Your precepts and Your judgments."[1]

We come before You once more, seeking Your forgiveness and mercy. You, O God, are our only hope. Hear our prayer and, for Your honor's sake, shine Your face upon this nation.

Give our leaders the desire to seek your wisdom and the courage to follow your guidance ... and watch over the men and women of our armed forces as they sacrifice for the cause of freedom.

We give you thanks for all You have done for us, and we earnestly pray that You will help us become, once again, a nation whose God is the Lord.

In the name of Your Son and our Savior we pray this prayer.

Amen.

CHAPTER 12

THE WEAPONS OF OUR WARFARE

DAVID BUTTS

One of the key reasons for prayerlessness in the Christian life is a theological one. Deep inside, many Christians believe that prayer really doesn't matter; God is going to do whatever He is going to do, and prayer isn't really going to change anything. If that is so, then why pray? Why spend time doing that which is ineffective for change? S. D. Gordon provides us with an answer: "The purpose of prayer is not to persuade or influence God, but to join forces with Him against the enemy."[1]

The Bible teaches that prayer not only changes the person who prays, it also changes situations. Scripture is filled with examples of people whose situations changed as a result of their prayer—whether on a personal scale, such as a Hannah praying for a son (1 Sam 1:9–18), or on a national scale, such as King Jehoshaphat praying for deliverance for Judah (1 Chr 20:1–23).

STANDING IN THE GAP

One of the best teachings on the power of prayer comes from Ezekiel 22:30: "I looked for someone among them who would build up the wall and stand before me in the gap on behalf of the land so I would not have to destroy it, but I found no one." This verse shows us the all-powerful Creator of the universe looking for someone to pray before He begins to act. The people of God had sinned and rebelled against Him and faced the punishment for their disobedience; in this case, the punishment was the destruction of the city of Jerusalem. But our merciful God was willing to delay or even avert this catastrophe if someone would intercede before Him on Jerusalem's behalf—if someone would "stand in the gap." God looked for such a person, but could find no one. Prayer could have made a difference then, and it still can today. God is waiting for us—His people—to stand before Him on behalf of our land (2 Chr 7:14).

The story of Moses praying on the hill while the Israelites fought the Amalekites (Exod 17:10-13) that we discussed earlier also demonstrates how prayer changes things: "As long as Moses held up his hands, the Israelites were winning, but whenever he lowered his hands, the Amalekites were winning" (Exod 17:11). Why would the position of an old man's hands have anything to do with the battle in the valley below? Lifted hands have always been a symbol of prayer. As long as God was involved through prayer, Israel won. In Exodus 17:16, after the battle, Moses built an altar to the Lord and said, "Because hands were lifted up against the throne of the LORD." Moses' lifting his hands wasn't just idle spiritual calisthenics; it was an expression of the power of prayer to change situations.

HIT OR MISS

Why did Jesus pray? Was it simply to change Himself? Or did Jesus know that prayer was the way His Father had chosen to work on this planet? Jesus didn't waste time doing things just for religious show. Jesus prayed because prayer was His way of staying in touch with His Father and it demonstrated His dependency upon His Father. When Jesus prayed, He *expected* God to act. His great high priestly prayer in John 17 demonstrated that He expected the Father to do things in response, both in His prayers as well as the prayers of His disciples.

Another one of the main reasons why so many Christians fail to pray or believe the wrong things about prayer is the seeming "hit or miss" aspect to much of our praying—sometimes it works, sometimes it doesn't. So we develop a bad theology to cover our misses and turn prayer into something it was never meant to be.

This problem happens when we look at prayer as a way of getting things from God. If we pray long enough, have enough faith, and get enough people to join us in prayer, maybe we'll get what we want from God. But prayer is not our way of getting things from God; prayer is God's chosen way of accomplishing His will on this planet. Our job in prayer is to draw near in intimacy. As we begin to understand a bit of the Lord's heart on a matter, then we begin to ask Him to accomplish what is already His will. It is at that point that prayer becomes a powerful change agent to achieve the Lord's purposes.

In spiritual warfare, it is prayer that keeps us connected to our commander-in-chief. Consequently, prayer becomes strategic in warfare. It is prayer that gives us our supply line of provisions for the battle. It is prayer that unleashes the power of God's Word to accomplish its purpose in overcoming the enemy. John Piper said it this way: "Until you know that life is war, we won't know what prayer is for."[2]

WEAPONS OF WARFARE

In a sermon, Charles H. Spurgeon preached:

> Like the Spartans, every Christian is born a warrior. It is his destiny to be assaulted, his duty to attack. Part of his life will be occupied with defensive warfare. He will

have to defend the *faith once delivered to the saints*. He will have to resist the devil. He will have to *stand against all the devil's wiles, and having done all, still to stand*. He will, however, be an ineffective Christian, if he acts only on the defensive. He must be one who goes against his foes, as well as [one who] stands still to receive their advance. He must be able to say with David, "I come to thee in the Name of the Lord of Hosts. The God of the armies of Israel, whom thou has defied" (1 Sam 17:45 [KJV]).

The weapons we fight with are not the weapons of the world. On the contrary: they have divine power to demolish strongholds (2 Cor 10:4).[3]

We are in a war like no other. Because it is spiritual warfare, the weapons that we use cannot be the normal weapons of this world. The devil does not succumb to guns or bombs. Nor does he surrender to human wisdom or strategies; to fight the devil, we need spiritual weapons.

Jesus offered an example of spiritual weapons in use when He resisted the devil in the wilderness. Whenever the devil tried to tempt Him, Jesus replied by quoting from Scripture (e.g., Matt 4:1-11). With every thrust of Satan's sword of lies, Jesus parried with the sword of the Lord—God's Word. Even the Son of God did not leave spiritual warfare to His own strength of character or will; He instead fought the battle with the spiritual weapon of the Word of God. Jesus offers a model for us to follow in our daily battle; we should know the Word of God so well that when we are asked our opinion on anything, we naturally give God's.

On a very practical level, we can win this spiritual battle by using the Word of God and prayer. Prayer keeps us in communication with our commander-in-chief. As we pray, He directs us, guides us, protects us, and even shows us the parts of His Word that are needed for the victory at any given moment. Have you ever experienced the Spirit working as His Word comes to your mind at just the right time, for just the right purpose?

PREVENTING CASUALTIES

As children, we would have what we called "sword drills" in our church youth group. In contest form, we would try to respond to questions our leaders asked us with the correct Bible verse as quickly as possible. Though we saw it as a game, we were being trained for a very real war. The soldier who must learn to use a weapon in the midst of battle is an unfortunate one. How much better it is to be trained in the proper use of your weapon in the safety and security of a training camp with your comrades?

When Paul admonishes Timothy, "Do your best to present yourself to God as one approved, a worker who does not need to be ashamed and who correctly handles the word of truth" (2 Tim 2:15), he is clearly calling Timothy to engage in serious training in the use of the spiritual weapon of the Word. If we do not have a working knowledge of Scripture, we will likely become a casualty in this spiritual battle we are in. Remember, the best defense to warding off the attacks of the tempter is a good offense. And there is just no better offense against temptation than proper knowledge and use of the Word of God.[4]

Most Christians agree that studying and knowing God's Word is valuable. But we often fail when it comes to actually using the Word in warfare. This is where prayer comes in. We must learn to pray God's Word back to Him. Beth Moore explains this well in her book *Praying God's Word*:

> In Ephesians 6:10–18, Paul listed the whole armor of God. Only one piece of the armor is actually a weapon. ... The sword of the Spirit, clearly identified as the Word of God, is the only offensive weapon listed in the whole armor of God. Second Corinthians 10:3 uses the plural, assuring us we have *weapons* for warfare. What would the other primary weapon be? Perhaps additional weapons might be identified elsewhere, but I believe the other *primary* weapon of our warfare is stated right after the words identifying the

sword of the Spirit as the Word of God in Ephesians 6:17. The next verse says, "And pray in the Spirit on all occasions." I am utterly convinced that the two major weapons with divine power in our warfare are the Word of God and Spirit-empowered prayer.[5]

My wife and I often share with churches that the one thing that has changed our individual prayer lives is learning to pray the Lord's Word back to Him. My favorite way to pray is, "open eyes, open Bible." As I read through the Bible, I'm led again and again to pray about that which is clearly God's will. I find myself praying about things I had never considered praying about in ways I had never expected to pray.

All of us can do that; it doesn't require special training or aptitude. We simply open our Bibles and begin to pray about what we are reading. Sometimes it is a matter of asking the Lord to teach us, to give us understanding of His Word. Other times there are clear ways of praying the Word into our own lives or the lives of those around us.

When I travel to different churches, I am often asked to pray for local congregations. There are many beneficial ways that I could pray over a congregation. But what I love to pray is what I know God desires to bring about in that fellowship, so I often turn to Ephesians 3:14 and begin praying around the verse in my own words, personalizing and applying Scripture to a particular group:

> I kneel before you in prayer Father, from whom our whole family in heaven and on earth derives our name. I pray that out of your glorious riches you might strengthen this church with power through your Spirit in their inner being, so that you, Lord Jesus, might dwell in their hearts through faith. I pray that the brothers and sisters here, being rooted and established in love, might have the power, together with all the saints, to grasp how wide and long and high and

deep is your love, O Christ. And that they might know
this love that surpasses knowledge—that they might
be filled to the measure of all your fullness, Lord.

This sort of praying overcomes the enemy. It is not based on emotions or desires, but on the revealed truth of God's will in Scripture. It touches God's heart because it emerges from His heart.

It is scriptural praying that allows us to resist the enemy, much as Jesus did in the wilderness temptations. Peter writes in 1 Peter 5:8: "Be alert and of sober mind. Your enemy the devil prowls around like a roaring lion looking for someone to devour." In the previous chapter, he writes, "Therefore be alert and of sober mind so that you may pray" (1 Pet 4:7). In both verses, he commands believers to practice self-control. Self-control is needed if we are to pray with power and passion. And prayer is needed if we are to be successful in resisting the devil.

NATIONAL PRAYER

GREG LAURIE

Father,

We come to You to pray for our nation, the United States of America.

How You have blessed us through the years, Lord! We rightly sing, "America, America, God shed His grace on thee." Yet we see trouble in our culture today. We see the breakdown of the family, crippling addictions, and random acts of horrific violence.

Lord, we need Your help in America. In recent days, we have done our best to remove Your Word and Your counsel from our courtrooms, classrooms, and culture. It seems, as President Lincoln once said, that we have "forgotten God."[1] But Lord, You have not forgotten us! You can bless and help and revive our country again.

Scripture tells us that "righteousness exalts a nation, but sin is a reproach to any people" (Prov 14:34 NKJV). Lord, in Your mercy, we ask that You would exalt our country again. We have had a number of great awakenings in America. We have experienced times of refreshing and revivals that changed not only the spiritual but also the moral landscape. As the psalmist said, "Will You not revive us again, that Your people may rejoice in You?" (Psa 85:6 NKJV).

That is our prayer for America today, Lord. Send a mighty spiritual awakening that will turn the hearts of men and women, boys and girls, back to you. You have told us if we will humble ourselves and pray, and seek Your face and turn from our wicked ways, that You will forgive our sins and heal our land (2 Chr 7:14 NKJV).

Forgive us today, Lord, and heal this troubled land that we love so much.

We ask all of this in the name of Jesus Christ.

CHAPTER 13

EVERYDAY COMBAT READINESS

DAVID BUTTS

I once returned from a Christian conference so excited about prayer that I determined I would get up early the next morning and spend a significant amount of time praying. When my alarm clock went off at 5:30 a.m. (yes, God is up then), I got up and prepared myself for prayer. But no sooner had I begun praying when I had this overpowering urge to wash my car. My mind began to be filled with images of my dirty car and the hectic schedule for the day ahead that wouldn't allow me to get it washed. It became so overwhelming that I found myself getting off my knees and getting ready to go wash my car.

Then a question came flooding into my mind: "When was the last time you had an overwhelming desire to wash your car at 5:30 in the morning?" The answer, of course, was, never. Then where did the thought originate to quit praying and go wash my car? That morning, I began to realize that God wanted me to pray, and I wanted to pray, but the devil wanted me to wash my car. It made the decision to stay and pray very simple. Awareness of the enemy's attack was a key to victory in my prayer time that day.

RECOGNIZING REALITY

In Ephesians 6:18, Paul writes, "Be alert and always keep on praying." Alertness is a critical area for victory in spiritual warfare that Christians often ignore, to their grave danger. Scripture contains many commands in this area: Be alert, watch, be careful, and be on your guard. You might think the authors of Scripture believed we were in some sort of danger that required us to be constantly aware and alert. Yet so many of us wander through life totally unaware of the dangers that lurk on every side.

I believe that 90 percent of the battle in the area of spiritual warfare is simply being aware that a battle is going on in and around us. Look at this from the perspective of actual physical warfare. Can you imagine a group of soldiers in the midst of a battle forgetting where they are? Planes are flying overhead, cannons are firing, bullets are whizzing by, but they forget completely about the battle raging around them, pack a nice lunch, and take off across the landscape looking for a nice spot to picnic. Every now and then as they walk, one of them gets injured, occasionally one is killed, and they stop and ask, "How can such bad things happen to such good people?"

Do you recognize this question? What's your response to this group of lost soldiers? Would you accuse them of failing to comprehend reality? Yet we are the same as them when we wander through our days with no awareness of the spiritual battles around us.

THE GIFT OF AWARENESS

Ephesians 6 offers a wonderful gift for helping us walk in awareness: the armor of God (Eph 6:10-24). Growing up in the church, I heard about the armor of God many times. We preached it, taught it, analyzed it, and dissected it. We did everything except what the Bible told us to do—put it on.

Many years ago, when I finally understood what to do with the armor, I began putting on the armor of God every morning. Since then, I've trained myself to put on the armor daily as I begin my shower. When the water hits me, it serves as a reminder to begin to pray and put on my spiritual protection for the day. The third verse of the old hymn, "Stand Up, Stand Up for Jesus," offers another reminder: "Put on the gospel armor, each piece put on with prayer."

When I put on God's armor daily, I am reminded that I am in a battle. Awareness floods into my soul that I am awaking to danger that day. But even more, there is the quiet assurance that I follow the commander-in-chief of the Lord's armies; He has provided both victory and protection for me in the midst of the day's struggles. He has loaned me His very own armor. So I pray with great joy, gratefully accepting and clothing myself with His armor. Alert to the battle, prepared through prayer, I move through the day's battles not with fear, but with confidence in my Lord's victory.

Putting on the armor is also becoming clothed with Christ. Do you realize that every part of the armor corresponds to an attribute of Jesus? When we put on the helmet of salvation, we realize that Jesus' very name means "God is my salvation." The breastplate of righteousness reminds us that Jesus has become our righteousness. The fact that Jesus is the truth is hammered home as we put on the belt of truth. The Prince of Peace Himself reminds us to fasten to our feet the readiness of the gospel of peace. As we take up the shield of faith, we remember the Scriptures that speak of Him as the shield that goes before us. Wielding the sword of the Lord, God's Word becomes a natural, daily activity for those who follow the living Word of God.

BE PREPARED

James gives us some wonderful steps for combat readiness in James 4:7-8: "Submit yourselves, then, to God. Resist the devil, and he will flee from you. Come near to God and he will

come near to you. Wash your hands, you sinners, and purify your hearts, you double-minded." This passage from James
is boot camp for believers—basic training for those preparing
for battle:

- **Submit to God.** There should be no outright rebellion against God in our lives that would give the devil
  a foothold.

- **Come near to God.** This is a prayer life focused on intimacy with the Lord. This life of intimacy is a place of protection in the midst of warfare.

- **Wash our hands and purify our hearts.** This call to holiness is essential if we are to stand victorious.

In the midst of submitting to God, drawing near to Him, and
walking in holiness, we are able to resist the devil.

It is important to understand that we do not simply do these
things once and then leave them behind. Warfare is constant.
We are called to vigilance. Submission, intimacy, holiness, and
resistance to the devil will need to be a part of every day's prayer
life. Here are some further steps for practical preparation for
everyday warfare that need to be a part of your daily prayers.

- **Pray for protection.** It is appropriate to ask the Lord for
  protection each day for ourselves, our family, and others for whom we may have responsibility. This involves
  both spiritual and physical protection. It is dangerous to
  assume we are protected. God is concerned with our protection, and He wants us to ask in dependence upon Him
  (Ezra 8:21–23; Job 1:10; Psa 91; John 17:12, 15).

- **Pray for discernment.** In the midst of daily life, it is vital
  that we understand what is of the enemy and what may
  simply be the circumstances of life. When Paul wrote that
  "we are not unaware of [Satan's] schemes" (2 Cor 2:11), he
  implied that we have the ability to discern the hand of the
  enemy in the midst of life's happenings. This is especially

vital for a local church as they deal with individuals and circumstances that may be creating problems. "Lord, is this the hand of our enemy at work?" may be a most appropriate prayer.

- **Pray for opened spiritual eyes.** Paul wrote in 2 Corinthians 4:4 that the God of this age has blinded the minds of unbelievers. One of our most important prayers should be for God to remove the blindfolds from the minds of those whom we may have the opportunity to reach with the gospel of Jesus Christ.

- **Pray for blessing.** We have the wonderful privilege of praying God's blessing upon those in need. Whether it is for those in your own family or those on the other side of the planet, the prayer of blessing is an attack of light versus darkness. It is a word of hope in the midst of despair.

- **Pray for spiritual leaders.** There is an all-out attack by the forces of hell against spiritual leaders. We need to be praying for our ministers every day, as well as other leaders in our churches.

- **Pray for revival**. There is nothing that Satan hates like revival. An awakened church is his worst fear. As we pray daily for a great awakening of the body of Christ, we are doing great damage to the kingdom of darkness. One of the great moves of God's Spirit today is in calling the church to fervent prayer for revival.

- **Pray for completion of the task of world evangelism**. The advance of God's kingdom throughout the world continues as people from every tribe, tongue, and nation give their lives to Jesus. Our prayers must reflect and reinforce this great move of God against the forces of darkness.

NATIONAL PRAYER

ANNE GRAHAM LOTZ

Lord of the Universe. Lord of this planet. Lord of the nations. Lord of our hearts.

On this National Day of Prayer, we look to You...

> In the darkness, You are our light.
>
> In the storm, You are our anchor.
>
> In our weakness, You are our strength.
>
> In our grief, You are our comfort.
>
> In our despair, You are our hope.
>
> In our confusion, You are our wisdom.
>
> In time of terrorism, You are our shield.
>
> In time of war, You are our peace.
>
> In times of uncertainty, You are the rock on which we stand.

We make our prayer to You using the words of the prophet Daniel: O Lord, You are the great and awesome God, who keeps His covenant of love with those who love Him and keep His commandments. You are merciful and forgiving. You are righteous, but this day we are covered with shame because we have sinned against You, and done wrong. We have turned away from Your commands and principles. We have turned away from You.[1]

Yet You have promised, in 2 Chronicles 7, that if we—a people identified with You—would humble ourselves, pray, seek Your face, and turn from our wicked ways, then You would hear our prayer, forgive our sin, and heal our land.

So we choose to stop pointing our finger at the sins of others and examine our own hearts and lives. We choose to acknowledge our own sin—our neglect and defiance and ignorance and even rejection of You. This day we choose to repent.

In response to our heartfelt repentance, God of Abraham, Isaac, and Jacob, Father of Jesus Christ, in keeping with all Your righteous acts and according to Your promise, turn away Your anger and Your wrath from the United States of America. Hear the prayers and petitions offered to You on this National Day of Prayer, as we give You our full attention. Give ear, our God, and hear; open Your eyes and see. We do not make requests of You because we are righteous, but because of Your great mercy.

For the glory of Your name, hear our prayer, forgive our sin, and heal our land.

We ask this in the name of Your Son, Jesus Christ, who offers us salvation from Your judgment, forgiveness for our sin, and reconciliation with You through His own blood shed on the cross.

Amen.

CHAPTER 14

WEAPONS TRAINING: APPLICATION OF PRAYER

KATHY BRANZELL

I received a bottle of fancy lotion as a gift one Christmas. I chuckled as I noticed that there were directions on the back label (who doesn't know how to apply lotion?), but I took a closer look anyway—maybe this special lotion had to be applied a certain way. The directions read, "Apply liberally, being careful to cover all of the areas wherever you need it most, to restore balance to your life." Really? This must be some amazing lotion if it can moisturize my skin *and* restore balance to my life. On second glance, though, I noticed that it did not promise to moisturize, just balance.

My life probably looks a lot like yours does: busy. Time just seems to fly, leaving me wishing every night that I had more time for my friends and family. I have many responsibilities that I am grateful for: a husband, children, a home, ministry, teaching, writing, prayer and Bible study time, serving on boards of directors and committees. I thank God for His gifts and the opportunities to use them, but 24 hours just never seem like enough.

Can you relate to this? Am I the only one who is out of balance? I imagine you are nodding right now, maybe even adding things you never seem to be able to get done to my list. (I bet you wish you knew the name of this lotion so it could restore balance to your life, too.) Friend, we both know that no matter how much of that lotion I squeezed out of that tube, it was *not* going to balance out this crazy life.

But I know something that does restore balance to my life. It cuts through the chaos and helps me to prioritize and make decisions. It must be applied daily, even several times per day, lavishly—especially in areas where I need it most. It is the application of prayer. As Christians, we may believe—just as I did with the lotion—that we don't need directions for prayer. But most of us do not really know how to *apply* prayer. We might know how to pray based on the example taught to us by our family or church service, but we will always have a capacity to grow in our understanding and ability to pray and apply the power of prayer.

Even some of the most amazing prayer warriors will tell you that they do not comprehend the vastness of the power, passion, and profit of praying to an all-powerful, all-loving God. He bends down from heaven to hear our prayers, delights in hearing from His children, desires and knows what is best for us, and is waiting for us to ask for His help. No man or woman can comprehend the full meaning and benefit of prayer. But wherever you are right now, whatever you know at this moment, you can apply prayer. You can commit to pray like you're applying for help—as a request or as a person applies for aid or a job. And you can also commit to *apply prayer*—to achieve a result, to spread it thoroughly over your life, spending significant time and effort in the area of prayer so that you become relevant in all situations and circumstances.

APPLICATION

My formal compilation of the definitions and synonyms of the word "application" would look something like this: "The process of putting something into use diligently, with devotion and attention, therefore acknowledging its relevance and value in a specific area or for a specific task." My less formal explanation is this: "Prayer is our faithful response of action in every emotion, responsibility, relationship, or event in our lives."

Before we panic, cry, get angry, freak out, quit, blame, or feel guilty, anxious, or depressed, we pray. And then if we need to, we pray some more. Likewise, before we call a friend, celebrate, throw a party, or jump up and down, we pray (and then pray some more). The application of prayer includes praying in the joy-filled victory moments of life as well as the hard, bad-news days of life.

In Philippians 4:6, Paul writes, "Do not be anxious about anything, but in every situation, by prayer and petition, with thanksgiving, present your requests to God." He says something similar in Colossians 4:2: "Devote yourselves to prayer, being watchful and thankful." These verses direct us to the foundation of prayer application: faith.

We do not turn to prayer as one of many solutions; God is the solution. We pray in faith. And we are anxious about nothing; instead, we are thankful and faith-filled, that as 2 Timothy 1:12 says, "For this reason I also suffer these things, but I am not ashamed; for I know whom I have believed and I am convinced that He is able to guard what I have entrusted to Him until that day" (NASB).

The foundation of prayer application is to be convinced—to believe—that God is able and willing to do the very best thing in every matter that we entrust to Him in prayer. Proverbs 23:12 states, "Apply your heart to instruction and your ears to words of knowledge." It was not enough for me to just have my bottle of lotion; keeping it in a drawer in my nightstand was not going to help me in any way. Likewise, simply having knowledge about prayer, God, Scripture, or Christian history will not change your life; only applying this knowledge to your heart will make a significant difference.

Lessons One and Two: Pray at all times, and believe at all times.

People apply lotion in many different ways. Some people squeeze the lotion onto one fingertip, and others use the palms of their hands. Some people rub the lotion between both palms and then spread it on other parts of their body, but others put it directly on a specific area and then use their hands to massage it in. Likewise, there are many ways to apply prayer. Think about these two questions before you go any further:

1. What do you know about God?
2. What do you know about prayer?

Some people have been praying the same words or the same way all of their Christian lives, not realizing that there are many ways to apply prayer.

If you grew up in a praying home, your first prayers were probably a blessing or grace at the meal table. For some of you, it may have been the same prayer, same words, at every meal. Others may have experienced conversation-like praying that was specific to the day's events, needs, and blessings. Both types of prayer, said with a loving heart, are absolutely pleasing to God; it is a pause to acknowledge His presence at the table and a thankfulness to Him as the provider of what you are about to eat.

A second prayer you were taught was probably at bedtime. Again, it may have been a memorized prayer that you repeated every night or a different prayer every night that included requests, thanks, and any other things you wanted to make sure God knew about. I love to listen to a child's prayers; they are so sweet and honest, full of love and assurance that God is not only real and really listening, but the faith that He will do something about it. The first lesson we can learn from a child is this: Apply prayer immediately and in all situations. And the second lesson is this: Know that God is real, really listening, and will do something about it. For this lesson, we can find support from Psalm 145:19, which states, "He will fulfill the desire of those who fear Him; He will also hear their cry and will save them" (NASB).

It is important to remember that His response may not be the response you were looking for. It may not come in the timing you wanted or the way you wanted. I have always appreciated the many examples of how God answers prayer in addition to the simple "yes" or "no":

- "Later"

- "With hard work and perseverance"

- "Not for you, but someone else"

- "My grace is sufficient"

- "It is not for you to understand—I will reveal what I decide to show you"

- "Trust and obey"

- "My ways are not your ways, nor My thoughts your thoughts"

It's not usually a simple "yes" or "no" answer. Life is complicated, but God is complete. Most of what we face in life we could never answer just "yes" or "no"; there might be an explanation, research, experience, or other priorities that we have to achieve or learn first. But rest assured: God is omniscient and all-knowing. There is nothing that He does not know or has not seen; nothing escapes His attention. He does not get distracted, and no one can fool Him. He can even see beyond our actions and know the intensions of our heart. We, on the other hand, don't know many things.

Lesson Three: God knows all things, and He will do the right thing about it.

I received a phone call from an acquaintance whose child attended the same school as my daughter. She was furious and suspicious of our principal because he had been hard to contact and had not returned her calls, as he had been absent from school recently. As I listened to her vent, I was careful not to reveal any information that I had been told in confidence by my close friend, the principal.

"I have always liked and respected him, but this is unforgivable," she said. "He must not care about my daughter or the school anymore, since he was off interviewing for other jobs at other schools."

I asked her, "Do you know for sure he is interviewing at other schools?"

"Well, no," she replied, "but—"

I cut her off before she could continue. "Have you talked with him personally about your concerns?"

"Of course not. I told you I can't get ahold of him. But when I do, he'll be sorry he ever ignored my calls."

Knowing where the principal was and the personal tragedy that was going on in his life, I calmly asked, "Knowing his integrity and heart, could there be something that you don't know—a good reason that has nothing to do with interviews, or avoiding you, that is the reason behind all this?"

There was a long pause and then another question. "Why, what do you know?"

"I'm asking you to give him a piece of your heart instead of a piece of your mind right now," I answered. "I'm not at liberty to say what he has confided in me, but I would ask you to pray for him instead of condemning him."

A couple of weeks later, the principal shared with the staff and parents about his battle with cancer, and three days later, the newspaper reported the unexpected death of his son.

How tragic it would have been for this woman to heap coals of anger and accusation on this man who had just been diagnosed with cancer and was struggling over losing his son? How would she have felt then? How about you? Have you ever judged someone only to find out later that you were completely wrong? Have you ever spewed your hurt, disappointment, or anger at someone, only to regret every word of it? Have you ever said, "If I knew then what I know now"?

In Jeremiah 29:11-13, the Lord says, "For I know the plans that I have for you ... plans for welfare and not for calamity to give you a future and a hope. Then you will call upon Me and come and pray to Me, and I will listen to you. You will seek Me and find Me, when you search for Me with all your heart" (NASB). In situations where something is just not right but you don't know what it is, talk to God about it. When a friend is not acting like herself or you encounter gossip or speculation, talk to God. Tell God what you saw, felt, or heard, and then ask for His wisdom. Ask Him to show you where you can help. Ask Him to silence the gossip. Ask Him to supply whatever that person or situation needs.

If you feel that you are a victim of harshness, neglect, or hurt, tell God about the situation and pour out your feelings to Him. King David wrote great examples of this in the psalms. He often starts a psalm complaining—even tattling—to God about his enemies, woes, hurt feelings, and suffering. But by the end of the psalm, he is rejoicing in God's goodness and remembering His faithfulness and blessing.

Talking to God in prayer will keep you from feeling the need to go talk to other people. They, like my lotion, may promise to help you, but they do not have any real authority, insight, or power. Compulsion, corruption, and consumption are never the right response—in fact, they may make matters worse. Like my lotion bottle, these things make you believe that they can do something that is totally out of the realm of their ability. But they will not resolve the conflict you have with another person any more than that lotion will balance my life. God, on the other hand, can.

In times of trouble, we must face conflicts head-on with prayer; we must apply prayer liberally to restore the balance to our emotions, actions, and decisions. And we must remember this: God is real; He is really listening, and not only will He do something about it, but He, knowing all things, will do the right thing about it.

Lesson Four: Prayer gives us access to One who is immeasurably more than anyone we could ever reach for here on earth.

In times of struggle, we learn that prayer is our first, immediate response. It is not what we come to after we are all out of ideas or have tapped out our resources. If prayer comes first, we will not be at the end of anything. Prayer is the beginning of peace and resolution; it is reaching for joy. It puts feet to our faith, and it protects us from dumb decisions and regretful reactions. Prayer is a response of relationship with the one and only God.

Second Samuel 22 records a prayer of King David. I return to this passage time and time again when I am feeling the enemy advancing in an area of my life that involves my family, ministry, friends, community, or nation. It is a reminder to me of the victory that comes from crying out to one who can do immeasurably more than anything or anyone else on this earth could ever do. David's prayer concludes with these words:

> The LORD lives! Praise be to my Rock!
>   Exalted be God, the Rock, my Savior!
> He is the God who avenges me,
>   who puts the nations under me,
> who sets me free from my enemies.
> You exalted me above my foes;
>   from a violent man you rescued me.
> Therefore I will praise you, LORD, among the nations;
>   I will sing the praises of your name (2 Sam 22:47–50).

We are never out of God's reach. As the saying goes, "Don't tell God how big your problem is, but rather, tell your problem, your enemy, your mountain, how big your God is!" Nothing can give you the guidance, joy, understanding, strength, compassion, comfort, patience, or resources that God can. No one can even come close.

Lesson Five: Prayer is a respectful response to a relationship with God.

Matthew 6:8 states that our heavenly Father knows what we need before we even ask. This may lead you to question, "If God knows what I need and He loves me, why do I have to ask?" Remember this: Prayer is a respectful response to a relationship with God. And it gives us access to one who is immeasurably more than anything or anyone we could ever reach for here on earth.

Imagine this scenario: Your son comes in from school very angry, giving you the cold shoulder and slamming cabinets in the kitchen while you are sitting at the table. Finally, he breaks the silence with this disrespectful question: "Why didn't you buy me a yearbook? Everyone else got their yearbooks today, but I did not get one."

You are startled by this behavior and reply, "When did you ask me to buy you a yearbook?"

He replies, "I shouldn't have to ask you. I get a yearbook every year. You know they sell them, and you should have gone up there and bought it when they were selling them."

You then ask, "How was I supposed to know when they were selling them if you didn't tell me or ask me for the money to buy it?"

Then he delivers the final blow: "You just should, that's what parents are supposed to do."

We can't wait around for God to shower us with blessings without so much as a humble, respectful conversation about the desires of our heart—a hurt that needs comfort, a decision that needs guidance, strength for a trial, courage to overcome a fear. Yes, God knows we need it, but we need to humble ourselves and ask. Otherwise, we are no different than the bratty child.

Remembering to say thank you is vital. Perhaps we haven't received what we are asking for now because we weren't grateful for the last blessing. This is another lesson on ways we pray: Prayer is access to God, but we gain access for many different reasons. We may access God in order to praise Him for all that He is—for His unchanging attributes that makes Him the King of kings and Lord of lords. Or we may gain access in order to apologize, to confess our sins, to admit wrongdoings, and to seek forgiveness and cleansing. We also gain access for the sake of others, to take others to the throne of God in intercession. We pray heartfelt prayers, memorized or conversational, and we can tell God our hurt and concerns in a way that we are refraining from judgment and gossip, but simply going to the Father who knows all and has the authority to do the right thing.

But we should always remember to access God to thank Him for everything—for life and breath, for His creation and His love, for prayers answered "yes," and for His protection and wisdom when He answers "no." We must thank Him for family, food, our homes, education, jobs, transportation, communication, all of our opportunities, gifts, possessions, our church, relationships, our abilities. A respectful relationship realizes that access to someone does not mean you are constantly taking from them but never giving and never appreciative. I imagine that you would not be friends for long with someone who took, and took, and took from you but never gave so much as a "thank you," much less anything else. That is not a relationship. As Galatians 4:6–7 says, "Because you are sons, God has sent forth the Spirit of His Son into our hearts, crying, 'Abba! Father!' Therefore you are no longer a slave, but a son; and if a son, then an heir through God" (NASB). God is our Father, we are His children and heirs (Rom 8:16). When we abide in Him, amazingly, He calls us friend.

Saying thank you has become one of the main aspects of my prayer life. I wake up and thank Him for another day of life and opportunities to know Him and make Him known. I lie down at night and thank Him for His covering through that day, for the people I saw, for a safe place to sleep. If you are ever short on things to pray over, just think through your day or turn on the news.

In stretching the idea of our "prayer life" as going beyond simply having a prayer time, we learn to pray beyond our urgent needs and pray in praise, confession, thanksgiving, intercession, and requests. These prayers may consist of one or two words; we may pray "wow!" at a sunset or "help me" at the sight of a temptation. Our prayers may be a song, a poem, or a speechless cry, or a sobbing groan. Entering into God's presence in prayer means bringing Him into your heart and mind. You are always already in His.

Lesson Six: The humble prayers of the faithful always result in gain and glory.

Second Chronicles 7:14 offers an important lesson in prayer: "If my people ... will humble themselves and pray and seek my face and turn from their wicked ways, then I will hear from heaven, and I will forgive their sin and will heal their land." The humble prayers of the faithful always result in gain and glory. Thankfully, God knows what we need and watches over us day and night; He never leaves us or forsakes us (Heb 13:5). When we approach God in prayer, we can always count on attaining something. God, in His wisdom, knows what we really need (not necessarily agreeing with what we want), and He is faithful to provide.

Like a good parent, God does not throw open the storehouses to spoil us rotten, but He enjoys rewarding us. He commands and rewards obedience, and He is satisfied when we listen to His guidance and follow it. He loves a cheerful giver, and He gives to those who are content with what they already have. He lifts up the lowly and brings down the proud; He disciplines those He loves. We may not receive that for which we came, but what He gives is better gain.

In John 15, Jesus teaches us that we cannot bear good fruit if we do not abide in Him, and that apart from Him we can do nothing (John 15:4–5). In John 15:7–8, He says, "If you abide in Me, and My words abide in you, ask whatever you wish, and it shall be done for you. By this is My Father glorified, that you bear much fruit, and so prove to be My disciples" (NASB). When we abide in Christ, we can come to God in prayer, and whatever we ask will be done for us. That is exciting news!

If we are truly abiding in Christ and His Word, we will not wish for selfish, sinful, prideful things, but rather godly opportunities and blessings. This is not to say that we will all walk around in sackcloth with nothing to eat in a humble hut; God says that He is glorified in His generosity to us. We must make sure that we are good stewards of His blessings, always knowing we are blessed to be a blessing, and to give Him credit for all that we have and do. It should be our desire to glorify God in all that we do and say, and that includes our prayers.

I will never forget the day that I sat reeling in the doctor's office with the words "brain tumor" ringing in my ears. *How could this be?* I thought. *I have a baby. I am young. I'm a Christian.* When I tried view it as being caused or justified by anything I was or did, I couldn't comprehend it. But I was not the center of the circumstance—it was not about me. It was only when I set my heart and mind on making God central that I began to gain understanding. I came to recognize that the peace I felt when I should have been overwrought with anxiety and the joy I experienced when the world said I should be in tears were a result of God's love and faithfulness as I prayed to Him through every test, scan, appointment, treatment, disappointment, and victory.

I have wept through my prayers, hardly able to speak or think clearly. I have prayed on my knees with my face in the floor. I have prayed with my arms in the air and while standing, sitting, or lying down. I have whispered, and I have raised my voice. I have even jumped on the bed with great joy, praying out praises and thanksgiving. All of these are acceptable ways to pray.

All those around me at that time—doctors, nurses, lab techs, radiologists, receptionists, other patients, friends, family members, and neighbors—heard me talk about God, the relationship I have with Him, His love, His presence, and His plan. They heard me speak of how He brought me through the first time, second time, and a third time. The story only continues as God and I continue to journey together using this tumor as a ministry tool that I desire to use for His glory.

Don't get me wrong, I beg Him to take it from me, just as Paul asked God to remove the "thorn in [his] flesh" (2 Cor 12:7). And as Paul knew, I know that God's grace is sufficient if He decides that it is not His plan to release me from it. In my prayers, He has given me the strength to say, "God knows what He is doing, He loves me, and so I know what He is doing is good." I would rather continue in pain for His gain than be released at the loss of His glory.

This is the application of prayer: that God be glorified by the faithfulness of His followers' prayers. It is putting feet to our faith. It is lifting up our prayers and then walking in faith that we have been heard by a loving and mighty God who plans on doing something loving and mighty. It is getting out of bed every morning focused on God's plans for the day and not the problems.

We must know God so that we know how to approach Him in prayer and apply the faith of those prayers to our everyday lives. Our prayer time becomes a prayer life when we continually take all that we know about Him and apply it, liberally, through our prayers. God shows the world, not just His followers, His awesomeness when He answers our prayers and we glorify Him when we pray.

Our faith is grown in our relationship with Him. When we learn about Him through His Word, experience fellowship and worship with other believers, listen to teachers and preachers talk about Him, see Him in His creation, and look for Him in the small things of our daily routine, we learn about Him. The big miracles of His forgiveness, healing, and bringing us through our trials also teach us about our Father. He is truly good all the time. May we always see it, and may the world always see it through our lives to His glory.

Lesson Seven: Pray without ceasing.

First Thessalonians 5:17 provides us with one final lesson on prayer: "Pray continually." Prayer without ceasing is the right amount of application that we need and God desires.

In all times, in all ways, we need to be in prayer. Whether we are praising Him, thanking Him, confessing our sins, proclaiming His goodness, sharing our hurts or happiness, we need to pray. Pray when you feel that God is prompting you, when He brings someone to your mind or a situation to your attention. Pray through heartache or when you receive your heart's desire. Pray when you see Him in His creation or when you need to be reminded that He is in control. Pray through any and every emotion and situation that comes your way. From your first thought in the morning to the last thought of the day, pray.

NATIONAL PRAYER

JACK GRAHAM

Heavenly Father,

We come to You in the Name that is above every name — Jesus Christ, our Lord and Savior. Our hearts cry out to You.

Knowing that You are a prayer-answering, faithful God — the one we trust in times like these — we ask that You renew our spirits, revive our churches, and heal our land.

We repent of our sins and ask for Your grace and power to save us. Hear our cry, oh God, and pour out Your Spirit upon us, that we may walk in obedience to Your Word.

We are desperate for Your tender mercies. We are broken and humbled before You.

Forgive us, and in the power of Your great love, lift us up to live in Your righteousness.

We pray for our beloved nation. May we repent, and return to You, and be a light to the nations. And we pray for our leaders and ask that You give them wisdom and faith to follow You.

Preserve and protect us, for You are our refuge and only hope.

Deliver us from all fears except to fear You, and may we courageously stand in the truth that sets us free.[1]

We pray with expectant faith and grateful hearts.

In Jesus' name, our Savior.

Amen.

CHAPTER 15

THE WARRIOR: ANSWER THE CALL

JOHN BORNSCHEIN

I n the 1950s, Americans were determined to return to our roots as a republic built on biblical principles. The USSR (present-day Russia) was claiming many of the same values as the United States. Thus, we had to set ourselves apart. This dilemma forced us to reexamine who we were as a people and identify the source that united us as the greatest nation on earth. Our firm faith in God was the defining factor, and Congress agreed, establishing an annual National Day of Prayer in 1952. Two years later, the words "under God" were added to the Pledge of Allegiance, and in 1956, "In God We Trust" was adopted as our national motto.

But in 1962, prayer was removed from public schools. Less than a decade after a series of major victories, the enemy hit us where it hurt—our children. That year, the US Supreme Court ruled against official prayer in public schools, opening the floodgates to a completely secular approach to public education in subsequent years:[1]

- Voluntary prayer was forbidden.

- Inclusion of Scripture was terminated.

- Classes on religion were halted.

- The Bible was eradicated from school libraries.

- Displays of the Ten Commandments were removed.

- Religious artwork was covered.

- Religious content in student papers or speeches was forbidden.

- The Bible was prohibited in classrooms.

So what happened next?

- SAT scores plummeted.

- American high school students regularly finished last, or near the bottom, in math and science testing.

- Crime in public schools and throughout the nation has escalated.

- Pregnancy rates in schools skyrocketed.

Gatherings of corporate repentance and humility before God are part of America's Judeo-Christian heritage. Since 1789, the president of the United States has called the nation to prayer more than 134 times.[2] Just as the sons of Issachar understood the signs of the times and sought the Lord's wisdom for the course to take as a nation (1 Chr 12:32), Christian leaders in America need to call the people back to the foundations of the faith. A solemn assembly is needed today more than ever. The cultural landscape is changing dramatically, and the negative impact to the family could have generational consequences. As E. M. Bounds wrote, "We need the spirit of Sunday carried over to Monday and continued until Saturday."[3] This can only be accomplished by leaders who pray.

The prophet Joel (850 BC) called the nation of Israel to assemble and "return to the LORD your God" (Joel 2:13). When a nation faces turbulent times and obstacles that seem insurmountable, there is no more important time to seek the Lord. In 1974, church leaders united in Lausanne, Switzerland, and again in 1989 in Manila, the capital of the Philippines, to refocus and realign the evangelical community in obedience to the Great Commission.[4] Now the National Prayer Committee is calling for leaders to unite as never before in prayer on behalf of America, seeking transformation and healing (2 Chr 7:14).

As E. M. Bounds stated in his powerful book *The Weapon of Prayer*:

> These days of ours have sore need of a generation of praying men, a band of men and women through whom God can bring His great and His greatest movements more fully into the world. The Lord our God is not straitened within Himself, but He *is* straitened in us, by reason of our little faith and weak praying. A breed of Christian is greatly needed who will seek tirelessly after God, who will give Him no rest, day and night, until He hearken to their cry. The times demand praying men who are all athirst for God's glory, who are broad and unselfish in their desires, quenchless for God, who seek Him late and early, and who will give themselves no rest until the whole earth be filled with His glory.[5]

Now is the time to stand firm and arise as the Christian soldier you have been called to be. Don't let fear hold you back. God can use you right now—today. You lack nothing that He can't provide.

IMAGE OF A WARRIOR

Let me paint a picture for you of the kind of warrior God uses in His army. Moses was a Levite, born around 1520 BC. Approximately 430 years passed from the time God gave His covenant promise to Abraham to the time He enacted the law through Moses (Gal 3:17). Moses played one of the most vital roles in the redemption of humanity. As the administrator and enforcer of the law, he enacted a system that would not be fulfilled until 1,500 years later by God's perfect design. But Moses wasn't so willing to assume this role (similar to many of us who are called into ministry).

From birth, Moses had been selected by God to save the nation of Israel and lead the people into the promised land. In Exodus 2, all of the Hebrew male infants were taken from their families and brutally thrown into the Nile River to drown. God saved Moses, though, who was taken into Pharaoh's palace to be raised as royalty. But Moses rejected his lofty position because he identified with and cared for his people. One day after witnessing an Egyptian abuse a fellow Hebrew, Moses killed the Egyptian and buried his body in the sand (Exod 2:11-12). When Pharaoh heard of this, he sought to kill Moses, but Moses escaped to the land of Midian.

Soon after he arrived in Midian, Moses came to the rescue of the daughters of Jethro, who were tending their father's flock and had been driven away from a local well by some troublesome shepherds. By now, we have a sense that Moses was frustrated by injustice and had a heroic nature that got him into trouble. Perhaps he was hotheaded and quick tempered. It is difficult to say for sure, but there is no doubt that Moses had little patience for evil and was quick to take matters into his own hands.

After marrying Zipporah, one of Jethro's daughters, Moses was blessed with a son, Gershom (Exod 2:22). He had a new home and family, and he made his living tending sheep, as was common for the people of Midian. At this point, God chose to intervene again, calling Moses to do what had never been done: deliver an entire nation from slavery and oppression. Moses should have been eager to do whatever God asked of him—after all, he owed his very life to God. But as we know from the biblical account, Moses was more than a little reluctant to accept the role God had for him.

One day, while Moses was in the desert tending Jethro's flocks, God spoke to him from a burning bush, reminding Moses of the suffering in Egypt and telling him of His intent to rescue the Hebrews and bring them into the promised land. It was a grand and amazing plan. Then God said, "So now, go. I am sending you to Pharaoh to bring my people the Israelites out of Egypt" (Exod 3:10). Moses was approximately 80 years old at the time.

Instead of agreeing to God's plan in humility and obedience, Moses insisted that he was the wrong man for the job, saying, "Who am I that I should go to Pharaoh and bring the Israelites out of Egypt?" (Exod 3:11). God assured Moses of His presence, promising him a sign, telling Moses His name, and describing the miracles He would perform to make the Egyptians listen. But Moses continued asking questions: "What if they do not believe me or listen to me and say, 'The LORD did not appear to you'?" (Exod 4:1).

At this point, God gave Moses two miraculous signs to perform. First, Moses threw his staff on the ground, and it became a snake. When the Lord commanded him to pick up the snake by the tail, it turned back into a staff. Then Moses placed his hand inside his tunic and when he brought it out again, it had become leprous. But the hand was miraculously restored when he placed it back inside his cloak. God then said that he would enable Moses to turn the waters of the Nile to blood if the people still refused to listen.

But Moses continued with his excuses, replying, "Pardon your servant, Lord. I have never been eloquent, neither in the past nor since you have spoken to your servant. I am slow of speech and tongue" (Exod 4:10). God assured Moses that He would give him the words to speak and teach him what to say, but Moses again tried to convince God that he was not the man for job: "Pardon your servant, Lord. Please send someone else" (Exod 4:13). In anger, God proposed yet another solution: He would have Aaron come alongside Moses to speak for him, but Moses would still perform the miracles God had given him.

Moses finally relented, agreeing to obey the Lord's command, and the rest is history.

OVERCOMING WEAKNESS

Why did Moses resist obeying God's command? He was afraid, unwilling to adjust his life to God's plan, and in great doubt of his own ability. But wasn't he also in doubt of *God's* ability? This entire discourse emphasizes God's ability and power; God wasn't asking Moses to perform this feat in his own ability or strength, but to simply be an instrument in God's hand.

Moses was afraid and used his own limitations as an excuse for not being up for the job, but there was an underlying issue here as well: a refusal to trust God or entrust himself to God, and perhaps even some bitterness about the past. Moses had been sure of himself years earlier, thinking he was called to deliver his people, but he did it in his own strength and failed. He might have been a bit angry with God over this because the Lord didn't use him the way he thought He should.

Moses' many excuses could have been a smoke screen—not just for lack of confidence in himself (though that was clearly a factor), but a lack of confidence in God and a refusal to trust Him. First he insisted that he was unworthy, and then he claimed that he lacked authority. Moses was afraid that the people would distrust him, and he used his speech impediments as a crutch. Finally, he just cowered in fear at the prospect of doing this seemingly impossible task, despite the presence of the Lord Himself. He gave one excuse after another:

- self-doubt
- lack of authority
- fear of rejection
- fear of public speaking
- fear of the overall assignment

Each time, God countered these fears with viable solutions. He countered Moses' self-doubt with the assurance that He would be with Moses. He countered Moses' lack of authority with His very name—like a king's signet ring. He countered Moses' fear of rejection by giving him the ability to perform miracles. He countered Moses' fear of public speaking with the assurance that He would be with Moses every step of the way to put the words in his mouth. Finally, he countered Moses' overall fear of the assignment by designating Aaron as his personal assistant, a man who would be his confidant and helper.

The fact that God was speaking to Moses directly was not enough; this recorded dialogue shows us that even the chosen were fearful. They were not machines, impervious to human emotion. Christ Himself suffered from the fear of torture and pain that He would experience on the cross. In the midst of his anguish, He prayed, "Father, if you are willing, take this cup from me" (Luke 22:42). Even Elijah, a mighty prophet of the Lord, was overwhelmed with fear when Jezebel put a bounty on his head. As 1 Kings 19:3-5 states, "Elijah was afraid and ran for his life. ... He came to a broom bush, sat down under it and prayed that he might die. 'I have had enough, LORD,' he said. 'Take my life; I am no better than my ancestors.' " In Genesis 32:1-12, we see Jacob trembling in fear in anticipation of meeting his brother, Esau, for the first time since stealing his birthright and blessing. Yet on this same journey, Jacob wrestled fearlessly with the living God and received a blessing.

Hebrews 11, also known as "the faith chapter," tells of men and women of faith who stood firm in the face of persecution and death, even though they never saw God's promises come to pass in their lifetimes. Yet each of these faithful believers had weaknesses, made mistakes, and experienced fear and other human emotions even though they had faith in God.

GOD'S RUBRIC

The story of Moses reminds us that God often selects men and women who appear unqualified in the eyes of the world to perform great and mighty deeds in His power. Other people probably would not have chosen these individuals because of their weaknesses or limitations. David is an excellent example of this.

When the Israelites demanded a king so they would be like other nations, God appointed the prophet Samuel to select the first king of Israel and directed him to anoint Saul. The Scriptures say that Saul was a head taller than any of the other Israelites (1 Sam 9:1–2). Even Samuel was in awe of his stature and said, "Do you see the man the LORD has chosen? There is no one like him among all the people" (10:24).

But King Saul turned away from the Lord and made decisions that brought God's judgment upon the entire nation (1 Sam 15). So God intervened and selected another king, whose heart was fully committed to Him. He didn't pick the obvious choice, either. First Samuel 16:6–8 records that when Samuel arrived at the home of Jesse (David's father) on God's command, he "saw Eliab and thought, 'Surely the LORD's anointed stands here before the LORD.' But the LORD said to Samuel, 'Do not consider his appearance or his height, for I have rejected him. The LORD does not look at the things people look at. People look at the outward appearance, but the LORD looks at the heart.' "

David wasn't even in the room with his brothers at the time. His father, Jesse, thought one of the other seven brothers would make a fine king because they were tall, well spoken, and distinguished looking. They were the perfect specimens—perfect for leadership. But God knew they were not the right ones for the job. Samuel asked Jesse if he had any other sons, and Jesse sent for David. As soon as David entered the room, Samuel anointed him king of Israel. This young shepherd boy would become one of the greatest kings the world has ever known.

God has selected other unlikely people to serve Him. The apostle Paul told Timothy to stay strong and persevere, adding,

"Don't let anyone look down on you because you are young, but set an example for the believers in speech, in conduct, in love, in faith and in purity" (1 Tim 4:12). Timothy probably struggled with issues of authority because, as a young pastor, he had to teach and reprimand older men. Paul sensed these fears and affirmed him. It is no wonder that Paul wrote:

> Brothers and sisters, think of what you were when you were called. Not many of you were wise by human standards; not many were influential; not many were of noble birth. But God chose the foolish things of the world to shame the wise; God chose the weak things of the world to shame the strong. God chose the lowly things of this world and the despised things—and the things that are not—to nullify the things that are, so that no one may boast before him (1 Cor 1:26–29).

Even the disciples that Christ handpicked were looked down upon because they were not educated men. But because they had no personal claim to their knowledge or authority, they were able to exalt Christ and His authority in their testimony about Him. Their weakness was their strength.

The point is this: When Moses laid his fears before the Lord, he was speaking on our behalf. Each of us would have trembled as well at the Lord's assignment. Moses was just bold enough (or scared enough) to voice what we ourselves would have felt. The same is true for other biblical heroes. They all had fears and doubts, but God was their strength and confidence. When we look at their accomplishments, we know that God was the source of their power, not their education, their heritage, their wealth, or their stature.

If God could use these men, He can use us. In Christ, we are cleansed and forgiven, thoroughly equipped through the Holy Spirit to do mighty things for God.

RISE TO THE CHALLENGE

Did you know there are more than 300,000 Bible-believing churches and clergy in America?[6] There are plenty of resources to get the job done, and the harvest is ripe. This is an exciting time in ministry because economic challenges mean that we have to work together. But if we are not intentional, we will lose all the ground won for us by the saints who have given their very lives for the religious freedoms we have today. God has called each of us to be watchmen on the wall for such a time as this. Are we complacently resting on the laurels of our patriarchs and matriarchs, or are we running with the torch that has been handed to us to bring light to a dark world? Stand in the gap on the front lines of the battle! God can change a nation through you.

How do we advance from here? What can we do as the chosen people of God? We can pray without ceasing. We can refuse to abdicate our responsibility and instead ask the Father for the courage of Elijah and Daniel. We can ask for the boldness of Peter and hold up the arms of our fellow soldiers, just as Aaron and Hur held up the arms of Moses (Exod 17:11–12), for the victory is ours in Christ Jesus (Rom 8:37). We must hold the line!

When an eagle battles against a snake, he grabs hold of it and takes it to the air. Likewise, we must battle this present darkness through the power of prayer. The prophet Isaiah knew the days would come that God's appointed would have to intercede for the sins of the people to preserve the nation—just as Moses had to do for the sins of Israel:

> And your righteousness will go before you;
>   The glory of the LORD will be your rear guard.
> Then you will call, and the LORD will answer;
>   You will cry, and He will say, "Here I am." ...
> Those from among you will rebuild the ancient ruins;
>   You will raise up the age-old foundations;

And you will be called the repairer of the breach,
The restorer of the streets in which to dwell
(Isa 58:8–9, 12 NASB).

Your obedience to become a prayer warrior is in response to the Holy Spirit's call to be the repairer of the breach!

God sent a reluctant prophet to Nineveh—a city wrought with debauchery, idolatry, and even child sacrifice. The heart of our God is that none should perish—but we must ask ourselves if we, too, have gone the course of Nineveh. Millions of babies have been aborted since 1973. In 2012, approximately 18 percent of all US pregnancies ended in abortion.[7] We call sexual immorality "diversity" and celebrate it as human expression while destroying the very foundations of the home. We have turned to idol worship in our culture, and we have called what is evil good and what is good, evil. Paul Harvey was right when he declared in 1965 that we have become a drug society, removing God from every aspect of our national lives—schools, businesses, media, government, and even churches.

There is a great breach in America today! We have turned our back on the living God and provoked Him to anger. He must execute His judgment, but we cry out to God on behalf of this nation that He would stay His holy hand and restore us back to Himself.

We do this that generations not yet born may praise and know the Lord. May it be our passion for God's people to unite in following His instructions in 2 Chronicles 7:14: to humble ourselves, pray and seek His face, and turn from our wicked ways, that He would forgive our sin and heal our land! We cannot rest while our nation is on a course to self-destruction.

We should be encouraged to stand boldly for God when we look to the valor of other men and women of God—such as Caleb from the book of Joshua. As a poem given me by a pastor friend states:

He stood before Joshua with flashing eyes;
"Give me this mountain before I die!"

> "But Caleb, you're old and the mountain is high;
> Choose a peaceful spot on this plain to die;
> The people who live on the mountain are strong;
> The battle you fight will be bloody and long."
> His eyes never wavered as he spoke without fear;
> "I've been promised this mountain for 45 years!
> And as for the people being mighty and tall;
> The bigger they are, the harder they fall!
> For it's not my strength on which I'm countin';
> For the Lord is going to give me that mountain;
> So let's quit talking while it is still light;
> For the Lord and I have a battle to fight!"[8]

You were chosen by God and out of obedience, you have answered. May He look you in your eyes one day and say, "Well done, good and faithful servant!"

Forge ahead, confident that you are a son or daughter of the King of kings! In faith and in the power of the Holy Spirit, you can move mountains. Be specific and watch God do an awesome work through you. Remember, Christ said you would do even greater things than He did through the power of the Holy Spirit (John 14:12). And as you engage in the battle on the front lines, let Psalm 91 remind you that the Lord Himself is our warrior:

> Whoever dwells in the shelter of the Most High
>   will rest in the shadow of the Almighty.
> I will say of the LORD, "He is my refuge and my fortress,
>   my God, in whom I trust."
>
> Surely he will save you
>   from the fowler's snare
>   and from the deadly pestilence.
> He will cover you with his feathers,
>   and under his wings you will find refuge;
>   his faithfulness will be your shield and rampart.
> You will not fear the terror of night,
>   nor the arrow that flies by day,

nor the pestilence that stalks in the darkness,
    nor the plague that destroys at midday.
A thousand may fall at your side,
    ten thousand at your right hand,
    but it will not come near you.
You will only observe with your eyes
    and see the punishment of the wicked.

If you say, "The LORD is my refuge,"
    And you make the Most High your dwelling,
no harm will overtake you,
    no disaster will come near your tent.
For he will command his angels concerning you
    to guard you in all your ways;
they will lift you up in their hands,
    so that you will not strike your foot against a stone.
You will tread on the lion and the cobra;
    you will trample the great lion and the serpent.

"Because he loves me," says the LORD, "I will rescue him;
    I will protect him, for he acknowledges my name.
He will call on me, and I will answer him;
    I will be with him in trouble,
    I will deliver him and honor him.
With long life I will satisfy him
    and show him my salvation."

The battle belongs to Him, and only in His power can we be victorious!

PRAYER

Heavenly Father, as Your servant I will go where You lead me. I dare not build the house without Your blessing, without You as my rock, my foundation. Direct my path, O Lord, and make clear the way in which I should journey. I have a deep burden for my neighbors, my community, and even my nation. My heart aches for what You must see. We have lost our way and have thrown dirt on Your mirror. Help me, Father, to unite Your people and lead them in life-changing prayer. Help us to understand the relationship You had with Enoch and walk in Your ways.

Truly, Father, I long to know You better. My soul thirsts for You. Give me a courage and passion that are contagious. Give me the words to speak and the tools to equip others. I know money is no barrier to You. I need only to cast my line into the water and draw up a fish to find the coin needed. Give me that faith. Help me to trust You when I am weak and tired. Please bring an Aaron alongside me to keep me lifted up when my heart is faint. At times I feel alone, but as you told Elijah, I know there are others whose hearts are committed to You.

Father, I humbly ask that You would bring people with a love for holiness into my life. May they have your heart to bring people together on holy ground. I need help and resources, my Lord. Prepare me for what You are about to do. Refine and cleanse me so that I may be Your instrument. I depend on You for all things, and I thank You for all You have provided. If You give me five talents, I shall make it five more with Your favor and blessing. In the name of Jesus, I pray, amen.

NATIONAL PRAYER

TONY EVANS

Dear heavenly Father,

We come to You today as a humble people desperate for Your supernatural intervention on behalf of our beloved nation. First, we thank You for all the blessings You have bestowed on our land, blessings that have allowed us to bring so much good and benefit to not only our own citizens but also to the rest of the world. The very ideals upon which this country was founded were based on biblical truths, no matter how some try to rewrite history to deny that very fact today.

This is why our hearts are so broken over how You continue to be marginalized and dismissed by both our people and our institutions. We are also saddened by the fact that Your people have contributed greatly to the spiritual apathy that now engulfs us. Our satisfaction in remaining religious without being fully committed to living out the truths of Your Word has caused us to become coconspirators with the forces of evil that are destroying us as a society.

It is for this reason that we personally and collectively repent of our carnality and recommit ourselves to becoming visible and verbal disciples of Jesus Christ. Enable us, by Your Spirit, to no longer be secret-agent Christians, but rather to publicly declare and live out Your truth in a spirit of love so that You feel welcome in our country once again.

Thank You for Your promise to hear our prayers when we call to You with hearts of repentance and obedience, which is how we are appealing to You today, Father. On behalf of Your church, we affirm afresh the priority You are to us, that You would fill every dimension of our lives as we seek to bring You glory through the advancement of Your kingdom in our personal lives, our family lives, and in the lives of our churches and our government leaders. We confidently invite heaven's intervention into all the affairs of our nation, and we praise You in advance for Your answer.

In Jesus' name we pray.

Amen.

A FIELD GUIDE FOR FAMILY PRAYER

ROBERT VELARDE
WITH JOHN BORNSCHEIN, ASHLEY BORNSCHEIN, LINDA RUTZEN, AND KARA SCHWAB

We all will face tough questions and situations when teaching our families about prayer as we seek to translate what we know into practice with our children and family members. This section will walk you through practical steps to take, Scripture passages for inspiration and reflection, helpful resources, and motivating ideas and encouragement designed to help families unite and witness the power of God.

WHY DO WE PRAY?

Your children may ask: Why do we pray? There are numerous reasons why we should pray. The following offer biblical support for our need for prayer. Read through them and underline these verses in your Bible to remind you why you ought to pray.

1. We are instructed to pray in the Bible. This is the primary reason we are to pray.

- Matthew 5:44
- Matthew 6:5
- Romans 12:12
- 1 Thessalonians 5:17
- James 5:16

2. Jesus prayed regularly. We should follow His example.

- Matthew 11:25–26
- John 17
- Luke 3:21
- Luke 5:16
- Luke 6:12
- Luke 9:18–28
- Luke 11:1

3. Prayer is how we communicate with God. Through prayer, we can worship and praise God, confess our sins and repent of them. We can also submit our requests, learn His will for us and seek His help.

- Philippians 4:6
- 1 Thessalonians 5:17

4. Through prayer, God allows us to participate in His works. Prayer plays a part in bringing others to faith in Christ. Prayer can heal nations and grant us strength to endure trials.

- 2 Chronicles 7:14
- Isaiah 40:29–31
- Hebrews 4:15–16

5. Prayer gives us power over evil. Physical strength and power are of no use in the spiritual realm. Even the physically weak can be strong in prayer.

- Matthew 26:41
- Mark 9:29
- 1 Timothy 4:8

6. Prayer is always available to us. Nothing can keep a believer from coming before God. Nations may condemn and forbid God's Word, but prayer has no barriers.

- Psalm 139:7
- Romans 8:38–39

7. Prayer keeps us humble before God. Through prayer we realize that God is in control and we can do nothing apart from Him.

- Jeremiah 32:17
- John 15:5
- Romans 8:28
- Colossians 3:12
- James 4:6–7
- 1 Peter 5:5–7

8. Prayer grants us the privilege of experiencing God. Prayer gives us an experiential basis for our faith.

- John 14:16–17
- Acts 1:3
- Acts 26:25

9. Answered prayer has the potential to be incredible witness to unbelievers. Skeptics will always have criticisms and doubts regarding answered prayer, but some will see the power of God at work and as a result, may be drawn to Christ.

- Colossians 4:2
- James 5:16

10. Prayer strengthens the bonds between believers. Scripture instructs us to pray for and confess our sins to one another. Through this process we come to better understand the needs of others and are able to empathize with them.

- 1 Timothy 2:1–2
- 1 John 5:15–16
- Jude 20

11. Prayer can succeed where other means have failed. Prayer is not a last resort, but it can often make a difference where other methods have failed.

- 1 Chronicles 16:11
- Proverbs 3:5–6
- James 5:13–15

PRAYING WITH YOUR CHILD FOR SALVATION

The most important prayer we can share with a child is the prayer of salvation. We need to be able to communicate God's message of love in a manner that children will understand. This message is simple enough for kids to comprehend, yet profound enough for scholars to ponder for a lifetime. God has taken the initiative in reconciling us to Him. Through the life, death, and bodily resurrection of Jesus Christ, He has shown us what infinite love is.

His Word tells us that everyone inherently has knowledge of two things: that He exists and that there are moral principles. Furthermore, the Bible goes on to tell us that we have fallen short of God's perfect standards. This sin, to use God's terminology, has short-circuited our relationship with our Creator. A holy and just God cannot allow sin in His presence. However, rather than leave us in this predicament of separation from Him, the Father designed a plan of reconciliation—He sent His Son, Jesus Christ, to pay the price for our transgressions.

This is the plan that we need to share with our children, and prayer is its foundation. Through it, we embrace God's provision of salvation through Jesus Christ. The significance of Jesus cannot be underestimated. As He said Himself, "I am the way and the truth and the life. No one comes to the Father except through me" (John 14:6). In addition, the apostle Peter said, "Salvation is found in no one else, for there is no other name under heaven given to mankind by which we must be saved" (Acts 4:12). Children must be given this understanding from an early age.

How to Lead Your Child to Christ

Things to Consider Ahead of Time

- Realize that God is more concerned about your child's destiny and happiness than you are. "The Lord is not slow in keeping His promise ... He is patient with you, not wanting anyone to perish, but everyone to come to repentance" (2 Pet 3:9).

- Beforehand, pray specifically that God will give you insights and wisdom in dealing with each child on his or her maturity level.

- Don't use terms like "take Jesus into your heart," "dying and going to hell," or "accepting Christ as your personal Savior." Children are either too literal ("How does Jesus breathe in my heart?") or the words are too cliché and trite for their understanding.

- Talk with each child alone, and don't be in a hurry. Make sure he or she understands. Discuss. Take your time.

A Few Cautions

When drawing children to Himself, Jesus said to *allow* them to come to Him. Only with adults did He use the term *compel*. Do not compel children. (See Mark 10:14 and Luke 14:23.)

Remember that unless God Himself is speaking through the Holy Spirit to the child, there will be no genuine heart experience of regeneration. Parents, don't get caught up in the idea that Jesus will return the day before you were going to speak to your child about salvation and that it will be too late. Look at God's character—He *is* love! He is not dangling your child's soul over hell. Wait on God's timing. Pray, with faith, believing. Be concerned, but don't push.

The Plan

Prepare ahead of time and know which Scriptures to use.

1. Tell your child that God loves him. Recite John 3:16. Recite it again with your child's name in place instead of "the world."

2. Remind your child that he or she needs the Savior.

3. Deal with sin carefully. Say that there is one thing that cannot enter heaven—*sin*. Be sure he or she knows what sin is. Ask your child to name some sins (things common to children—lying, sassing, disobeying, etc.). Sin is *doing* or *thinking* anything wrong according to God's Word.

- Ask, "Have you sinned?"
- If the answer is "no," do *not* continue. Assure your child that when he or she does feel like they have sinned to come and talk to you again. Some parents may want to have prayer, thanking God "for this young child who is

willing to do what is right." Make it easy for them to talk to you again, but do not continue. Do not say, "Oh, yes, you have too sinned!" and then name some. With children, wait for God's conviction.

- If the answer is "yes," continue. Your child may even give a personal illustration of some sin they have done recently or one that has bothered them.

- Tell them what God says about sin: We've all sinned. "There is none righteousness, no, not one" (Rom 3:10). "For all have sinned, and fall short of the glory of God" (Rom 3:23). Because of that sin, we can't get to God, "for the wages of sin is death" (Rom 6:23). So He had to come to us: "But the gift of God is eternal life through Jesus Christ our Lord" (Rom 6:23).

4. Explain that the gift of salvation is free. Relate God's gift of salvation to receiving Christmas gifts—we don't earn this gift or pay for it; we just accept it and are thankful for it.

5. Encourage your child to make a definite decision. Explain that Christ must be received if salvation is to be possessed but, remember, *do not force a decision.* Ask your child to pray, out loud, in their own words. Give them some things they could say if they seem unsure. It is best to avoid having the child repeat a memorized prayer after you; let them think, and make it personal.[1] Now be prepared for a blessing! After salvation has occurred, pray for your child out loud. Pronounce a blessing on them.

6. Explain to your child that God will never leave them. Show your child that one can keep a relationship open with God through repentance and forgiveness (just like family and friends) and that God will always love them. "I will never leave thee, nor forsake thee" (Heb 13:5).

7. Teach your child "family" responsibilities (the "Big Five").
Tell your child that they are now a member of God's family, and
therefore has some responsibilities as a family member: (1) to
pray, (2) to know more about God (reading the Bible), (3) to love
God's church, (4) to love others (the Golden Rule: "Do to others
as you would have them do to you," Luke 6:31), and (5) to give to
God's work.

If you wish, you can guide your child through the prayer. You
may follow this language, if you like:

> Dear God, I know I am a sinner [have child name spe-
> cific sins he or she acknowledged earlier, such as lying,
> stealing, disobeying]. I know that Jesus died on the
> cross to pay for all of my sins. I ask you to forgive me of
> my sins. I believe that Jesus died for me and rose from
> the dead, and I now take Him as my Savior. Thank you
> for loving me. In Jesus' name. Amen.

PRAYER AND YOUR TEEN

One dad recalls a meeting he had with other fathers about how
to communicate with young people about spiritual issues:

> I was involved in a "Rite of Passage" planning ses-
> sion with six other dads. Our conversation centered
> around how we could discuss spiritual concepts with
> our children, to prepare them to take their places in
> the church as godly men and women. However, several
> of the fathers stated they had never before talked with
> their children about spiritual matters.

You might understand the response of those men. Even if you
have carefully and conscientiously nurtured faith in your children through their early years, adolescence brings changes. As a
young child, your son or daughter may have accepted everything
you said without question. Now there seems to be nothing but

questions. In short, the season of "sermons" is over; the days of discussion have arrived.

The reason is simple: Teens want to be treated as adults. So, in order to talk with them about spiritual matters, we parents need to relate to our teens as grownups. The best place to begin is by building on the existing relationship.[2]

Building on the Relationship

1. Spending time with your teen. Time communicates value to teenagers; when we spend time with them, they know they are important to us. Teens want (and need) some privacy and space, but keep planning family activities that include them.

2. Listen more than you lecture. The time for instruction is mostly past; now, it's important to listen to our teens so we can better understand how they think. Listening creates opportunities to find out what they know, what they think, what they feel, and what principles guide their lives. Here are a few ideas to help you listen more closely:

- **Ask open-ended questions that start with words such as "how," "what," and "why."** For example: "When your prayer wasn't answered the way you wanted, how did you feel? Why do you think God answered the way He did?"

- **Ask your teens to define what's important in their culture.** Ask about particular words in songs or popular phrases they use.

- **Praise them for their accomplishments,** such as earning good grades, reaching a tough goal or making a hard decision that showed good judgment. Avoid the trap of seeing—and talking about—only their mistakes and shortcomings.

3. Express encouragement and affection, physically and verbally. We can show our support in simple ways: a hug, a pat on the back, a kind word or compliment. Just using good

manners can communicate love and respect, which are important to our young men and women. We can say "please," "thank
you," and "I'm sorry" to them as well as to anyone. Being our
children makes them no less deserving of our consideration.

4. Have fun together. A ballgame. A meal at a restaurant.
A drive in the country. Shopping at the mall. These are places where you can enjoy casual, nonthreatening conversations
and just get to know each other better. Here's one suggestion:
Schedule a weekly "date night" with your teen, with the understanding that it is for fun and will be free of heavy conversation.
But be sure to blanket your time with prayer in advance.

One father made a breakfast appointment with his teenage
son because he wanted to tell his son about the hopes, dreams,
and prayers he had for the boy. But the father also found out
that the son wanted more time—and breakfasts—with his dad.
Thus began a wonderful habit. Each week, father and son went
out for the breakfast, where they discussed spiritual issues and
other important things. But they also spent a lot of time talking
about sports. Communication comes easier when it is part of an
ongoing relationship.

5. Be vulnerable. Teens respect honesty, and being open with
them will encourage them to be open with us. Vulnerability is
not a weakness; it is part of being human. Our children need to
know we have problems, too. The good news is that our troubles
give us opportunities to talk with our teens about how to rely on
the Lord and his strength.

6. Live consistently. Values are caught, not taught. Teens
look for consistency between our words and actions, especially
when it comes to our relationship with God. So we need to ask
ourselves: How is my relationship with Him? What words would
the Lord use to describe my relationship with Him? How often
do I pray? What do I ask God for? What happens when I pray?

7. Learn about their world. Teens often think that adults are out of touch with the issues they face (and sometimes they're right!). One way to understand their world is to read some teenage magazines. Then we can follow up on our research by asking our teens' opinions on topics we come across. The more we know their world, the more we will know them.

8. Be a friend. One way we parents can show respect to our teens is to show sensitivity and other affirmation when they are having trouble. We need to resist the urge to tease them when they are bothered by something important to them, such as a relationship with the opposite sex. Ephesians 4:29 tells us that we should only say "what is helpful for building others up according to their needs, that it may benefit those who listen"—and that verse doesn't have an exception clause for our children!

9. Pray specifically for your teen at least once a week. We must set aside time to pray for our children. Some parents find it helpful to fast and pray for their kids one day a week. We can help our teens see the power of prayer when we ask them every week what we can pray about for them. They may be concerned about a tough exam or a friendship that's run aground. They might even talk about a temptation that they are struggling with.

At the end of the week, remember to tell your teen you were praying for him or her. Together, you will see how God answers your prayers.

Talking Spiritual

As your relationship develops, you will find more and more opportunities to discuss deep, spiritual matters. Here are some key topics and questions to cover—but don't be limited by this list. Be prepared to talk about any questions, doubts, or discoveries your teen has.

1. **Your teen's personal relationship with God:** Try asking your teen, "If God were to describe your relationship with Him, what words would He use? What makes you feel this way?"

2. **Purity and holiness:** Ask, "How would you describe 'purity' to your best friend? Why? When I say the word 'holy,' what comes to mind, and why?"

3. **Prayer:** Ask, "How does prayer fit into your daily life? If prayer is spiritual breathing, what chokes it out of your schedule? What is the biggest question you have about prayer?"

4. **Relationships:** As an icebreaker, you might say, "Describe a relationship between a boy and a girl that honors God. What limits are important for you to maintain in a relationship that glorifies God? Whom do you know that sets a good example in a boy-girl relationship? What makes it good?"

5. **Honor:** Ask your teen, "How do you honor a friend of yours? Why? How does that friend honor you?"

Talking in Your Teen's World

Parents can wonder if the teen in their family has come from another country—or maybe another planet. That's how hard communication can seem, even in the best relationships. How can you encourage open, honest discussion with your teen? Try some of these ideas.

1. **Plan your communication.** Good communication requires a proper mood and setting, as well as good timing. Some parents find that going for a long drive with their teen once a week is a great way to create discussion time. Not only is there a "captive audience," but your conversation may feel less intimidating because you are talking side by side, not face to face. The two of you may be in a much better position, literally, to have a great discussion.

2. Have a discussion—don't preach a sermon. A conversation is like a tennis game: To keep the match going, the ball must be hit back and forth. Rather than dictating conclusions or discounting their ideas, use questions and thoughtful responses to coach your teen's thinking and help them learn to think and speak clearly about important issues.

3. Engage them in nonthreatening, thought-provoking conversation. Ask your teen's opinions on different issues. Talk about the news you hear or read, or open a discussion about a TV program you watch together. Remember: If you respect your teen's opinions, it's likely they will respect yours (even if they don't say so).

4. Make it easy for your teen to be honest. One couple created a report card so their son and daughter could grade them on their relationship. It looked like this:

Dad (Mom) shows me he (she) loves me ___

Dad (Mom) is fair in his (her) decisions ___

Dad (Mom) is interested in my feelings ___

Dad (Mom) admits when he (she) is wrong ___

Dad (Mom) spends enough time with me ___

Dad (Mom) controls his (her) anger and words ___

Dad (Mom) listens to what I say ___

Dad (Mom) is fun ___

Dad (Mom) trusts me ___

Dad (Mom) respects me ___

Dad (Mom) enjoys being with me ___

Dad (Mom) provides spiritual leadership ___

Dad (Mom) makes me a priority in his (her) life ___

Overall grade ___

One a scale from 1 to 10 (10 is best), what kind of relationship do you want with Dad (Mom)?

On the same scale, where are you today in your relationship with Dad (Mom)?

If your Dad (Mom) could change three things to raise his or her grade to a 10, what would they be?

1.

2.

3.

In Deuteronomy 6:4–7, God instructs parents to teach children about following Him. In what three areas of your spiritual walk would you like your dad or mom to help?

1.

2.

3.

This approach opens the door for great conversations. But be careful when using this process. This isn't a time to defend your position; you can only ask questions to clarify a response. Remember: "Do not embitter your children, or they will become discouraged" (Col 3:21).

WHAT IF GOD DOESN'T ANSWER?

In his book *Why Don't I Get What I Pray For?*, John Cowart writes:

> If a fisherman who believes God answers prayer goes fishing early one morning and prays really hard all day to catch fish, but does not even get a nibble, what does that mean? Once, while interviewing some children for a newspaper article on kids' views of God, I posed this question to the group. The question did not faze

the seven-year-old theologians. "It's because the fish prayed harder," answered one little girl blithely.[3]

Why is it that sometimes we pray so hard for a specific thing, only to feel as though God has ignored us? It's a question you're likely to face when you're teaching your children about prayer—it often seems that our requests go unanswered. At times like these, is the Lord avoiding us, or are we missing something? Let's take a closer look at what we may be experiencing:

1. He always hears our prayers. Even when He is silent, keep praying! There are times when the lesson we need to learn is persistence. More than anything, the Lord desires a personal relationship with His people, and prayer is a significant part of this. He wants to comfort us and have fellowship with us. If He always answered our prayers immediately, exactly as we were expecting, there would be no need for us to spend time with Him. He is personal and wants us to come to Him whenever we have needs or hurts. Time in prayer should not be our last resort, but our first response. Some helpful verses for these times include Psalm 23:4; 119:76; 2 Corinthians 1:3-6; and 1 Peter 3:12.

2. God may answer our prayers, but it may not happen immediately. The Lord works in His way and in His time. One of the side effects of our fast-paced culture is that we often expect an instant response. But the Lord is not our servant. He will not be accountable to man; He is sovereign God. He never answered Job's excellent questions about his sufferings. James tells us that there may be times we are suffering in order to build endurance (Jas 1:2-4). If we become angry at God for allowing us to go through trials, we may miss what He would like us to learn through the experience. God teaches us through His Word, but we *learn* by applying this knowledge to the circumstances of life. Check out Isaiah 55:8-9 for more.

3. We may have a problem that is hindering our relationship with the Lord. Prayer is more than just asking God to do things—it's about a relationship. We need to consider that something may be interfering with our connection to the Lord. Of course, he still hears our prayers, and in His sovereignty He is certainly capable of answering the supplications of sinners. But there may be times when our behavior puts a wall between us and our fellowship with God (Psa 66:18). This is one of the reasons the apostle Paul used when warning certain Corinthians not to participate in the Lord's Supper (1 Cor 11:27-30).

4. Our prayer may not be in line with God's will. He knows what is best for us and will not always give us what we ask for. Simply put, we may be praying for something that is completely out of the will of the Lord. This is a difficult reason because His will in a given situation is not always clear. We are not to lean on our own understanding (Prov 3:5) but have faith in the fact that "God works for the good of those who love him, who have been called according to his purpose" (Rom 8:28). Even the apostle Paul prayed three times and God did not meet his request because He had other intentions (2 Cor 12:7-9).

5. God may be in the process of answering our prayer, but we are too preoccupied to notice. One thing we find in the Bible is that the Lord is full of surprises. There may be times when we are expecting a specific response to our prayer, but God has other plans for how He will answer us. We need to constantly be aware of what is going on around us and determine if the Lord is already at work on our behalf.

6. God knows us and will supply all our needs, not necessarily our wants. Prayer is not our ticket to "getting stuff" from God (Jas 4:3). There is no formula that we can follow that will guarantee the results that we are seeking. Certainly, the Lord may choose to bring material blessings upon us, but we must be careful of our motives. Matthew 6:19-20 reminds us to store up treasures in heaven, not on earth. If we are praying out of selfish desire, we can be sure that such behavior is not in line with the will of God.

7. Facts should drive our faith, not our feelings. We need to cling to His promises. Even though we may not see answers to our prayers, it is important that we have faith that God is working in our lives and has heard our supplications. Some of these promises to us are found in Joshua 1:5; Matthew 11:30; and 2 Corinthians 5:7.

Of course, this list is not exhaustive, but it does give us some reasons for why we sometimes have difficulty in dealing with God's apparent silence. It's also important that we keep in mind that there are no specific steps or keys to getting the Lord to answer our prayers the way we would like them answered. There is no "secret recipe" that will twist His arm and grant us complete and satisfying answers to our prayers.

In *Experiencing God*, Henry Blackaby states, "You can respond to the silence of God in two ways. One response is for you to go into depression, a sense of guilt and self-condemnation. The other response is for you to have expectation that God is about to bring you to a deeper knowledge of Himself."[4]

Ultimately, it can be said that there are only two answers to prayer: "Yes!" and "Trust Me!" As God's Word puts it, "We know that in all things God works for the good of those who love him, who have been called according to his purpose" (Rom 8:28). In other words, we need to *trust* Him even when we can't *track* Him.

In addition, we shouldn't always assume that there is a problem with us that is somehow restraining God's power. He loves us in Christ and wants what is best for us, in spite of our shortcomings. Our role is to seek to strengthen our relationship with Him. If we humbly come before Him and trust Him in our daily lives, He will bless our dedication.

In his book *When God Doesn't Make Sense*, Dr. James Dobson makes several astute observations on this topic. Perhaps it is best if we end this section with a portion of that text:

I've been trying to say with this discussion that our view of God is too small—that His power and His wisdom cannot even be imagined by us mortals. He is not just "the man upstairs" or "the great chauffeur in the sky," or some kind of wizard who will do a dance for those who make the right noises. We dare not trivialize the One about Whom it is written,

> "Praise be to you, O Lord, God of our father Israel, from everlasting to everlasting. Yours, O Lord, is the greatness and the power and the glory and the majesty and the splendor, for everything in heaven and earth is yours. Yours, O Lord, is the kingdom; you are exalted as head over all. Wealth and honor come from you; you are the ruler of all things. In your hands are strength and power to exalt and give strength to all. Now, our God, we give you thanks, and praise your glorious name."
> —1 Chronicles 29:10–13

If we truly understood the majesty of this Lord and the depths of His love for us, we would certainly accept those times when He defies human logic and sensibilities. Indeed, that is what we *must* do. Expect confusing experiences to occur along the way. Welcome them as friends—as opportunities for your faith to grow. Hold fast to your faith, without which it is impossible to please Him. Never let yourself succumb to the "betrayal barrier," which is Satan's most effective tool against us. Instead, store away your questions for a lengthy conversation on the other side, and then press on toward the mark. Any other approach is foolhardy—because your arms are too short to box with God.[5]

PRAYER: KEY TO RELATIONSHIP WITH JESUS CHRIST

Prayer ultimately brings us into closer relationship with not just our children, but most importantly forms the basis for a daily relationship with our savior, Jesus Christ. The benefits of following Jesus are numerous. God wants each of us to experience these wonderful blessings, if only we will come to Him in reverent submission. Below are several reasons why we should embrace a daily relationship with Christ.

1. A spiritual connection that will last forever. God wants you to experience His joy on a regular basis in this life as well as throughout eternity. When you accept Christ, you receive spiritual vitality through your daily relationship with Him.

- Psalm 16:11
- Jeremiah 31:3
- Matthew 25:46
- John 3:14–16; 3:36; 4:13–14; 5:24; 6:39–40; 10:27–28; 17:1–3
- Romans 5:21; 6:22–23
- 2 Corinthians 4:17–5:1

2. Assurance of God's unconditional love. Christ bridges the gap between you and God. Through a relationship with Jesus, you are assured of His unconditional love for you. No matter what you have done or will do, as long as you have a relationship with Jesus, God will love you. He is always present and ready to help those who put their trust in His Son.

- John 3:16; 16:27
- Romans 5:8; 8:35–39
- Ephesians 2:4–5; 3:17–19
- 1 Timothy 1:14
- 1 John 3:1; 4:7–10

3. Meaning and purpose in life. Through a relationship with Christ, we realize that God is intimately aware of every aspect of our lives. We can trust that He will guide and direct us as we submit to Him and pray that He will lead us. Things may not turn out as we would like them to, but we know that the Lord is in control and His will is "pleasing and perfect" (Rom 12:2).

Furthermore, Christianity is grounded in historical and rational truth. As the apostle Paul put it, our faith is "true and reasonable" (Acts 26:25). As such, it provides meaningful answers to the most difficult questions in life. This includes a coherent moral foundation that clearly indicates right from wrong.

- Acts 1:3; 26:25
- 2 Peter 1:16
- 1 John 1:1–3

4. Strength to face each day. Regardless of your circumstances, God will grant you strength when you seek His help. As you seek to serve the Lord, He will empower you to serve Him. Through difficulties will still arise, a firm foundation in Christ gives you the ability to face and overcome the challenges of life—everything from financial difficulties to dealing with family members and humanity in general.

- Isaiah 41:10
- John 16:33
- Philippians 4:13
- 1 Timothy 1:12
- 2 Timothy 4:17

5. Peace. God's peace does not exempt you from trials. Rather, it calms you and places your confidence in the Lord. As you experience difficulties and feel as though you are out of control, rest in assurance that God is sovereign and always in control (Gen 18:14).

- Psalm 29:11

- John 14:27; 16:33

- Acts 10:36

- Romans 5:1

- Ephesians 2:14–17

- Philippians 4:6–7

- Colossians 3:15

6. You become part of the body of Christ (the Church). When you receive Christ into your life, you become part of a worldwide family of believers. Through participation in a local Christian church, believers are able to support one another on a regular basis.

- Romans 12:4–5

- 1 Corinthians 12:13–14

CONCLUSION

While the needs in our family are often overwhelming, the opportunities to impact our loved ones with prayer are endless. God is continually working through the prayers of His people. May the prayers of the family of God go with you as you train up your children and family members in a life devoted to Christ!

FOR FURTHER STUDY

FEED THE SPIRIT

- John 3:16
- John 14:6
- Romans 5:8
- Romans 6:23
- 2 Corinthians 4–5
- Philippians 4:13
- Titus 3:5
- James 1:12
- Revelation 3:21

DRIVE THE MIND, DIRECT THE BODY

- Exodus 20
- Psalm 118:8–9
- Proverbs 3:1–7, 21–26
- Proverbs 7:1–4
- Proverbs 16:3–7

- Proverbs 24:10–12
- Ecclesiastes 3:1–8
- Matthew 4:4
- Matthew 5:16
- Mark 16:15–16
- John 14:15, 23
- Romans 12:1–2, 9–21
- 1 Corinthians 9:27
- 1 Corinthians 12:12–27
- Ephesians 4:29
- Philippians 2:3
- Colossians 3:23
- 1 Thessalonians 5:22
- 1 Timothy 4:7–8
- Hebrews 3:14
- Hebrews 13: 15–16
- 1 John 5:14–15

TAKE COURAGE! BE FOCUSED AND CONFIDENT IN HIM

- Deuteronomy 31:6
- Joshua 1:6–7
- 2 Samuel 10:12
- 2 Chronicles 32:7–8
- Psalm 56
- Isaiah 26:3–4
- Acts 4:13
- Hebrews 3:6
- Hebrews 10:35–36

RECOMMENDED MINISTRIES

ALLIANCE DEFENDING FREEDOM
http://www.adflegal.org
The Alliance Defending Freedom (ADF) works with other groups to confront the ACLU and other like-minded organizations to keep the door open for the gospel in America. In addition, it is their goal to restore religious freedom as it was originally envisioned by the framers of the US Constitution.

AMERICAN CENTER FOR LAW AND JUSTICE
http://aclj.org
The American Center for Law and Justice (ACLJ) is a public-interest law firm committed to ensuring the ongoing viability of constitutional freedoms in accordance with the principles of justice outlined in Scripture. As a public-interest law firm, the ACLJ is dedicated to the concept that freedom and democracy are God-given, unalienable rights that must be protected both domestically and internationally.

CALVARY FELLOWSHIP CHURCH
http://www.calvaryfountain.org
Calvary Fellowship has a unique vision for reaching and impacting communities through various ministry "touch points." During the week, it is a community center containing a teen center, an early learning center, and an event center. On weekends, hundreds of people gather together as the body of Christ. John Bornschein serves as the senior pastor.

CHRISTIAN LEGAL SOCIETY
http://www.clsnet.org
The Christian Legal Society's mission is "inspiring, encouraging, and equipping Christian lawyers and law students both individually and in community to proclaim, love and serve Jesus Christ through the study and practice of law, the provision of legal assistance to the poor and needy, and the defense of the inalienable rights to life and religious freedom."[1] As a national grassroots network, the society also advocates biblical conflict resolution and public justice.

CRUMILITARY
http://crumilitary.org
Cru (formerly Campus Crusade) joins with active and reserve military personnel, commanders, chaplains, and volunteers to help military men and women and their families in all nations gain spiritual readiness for life and their mission.

FACE FOR EDUCATORS
http://www.prayingeducator.org
Fellowship and Christian Encouragement (FACE) for Educators is an interdenominational Christian ministry serving public, private, and home educators. FACE is one of the fastest-growing Christian ministries in the United States, with prayer chapters motivating and encouraging educators throughout the United States and around the world.

FAMILY RESEARCH COUNCIL
http://www.frc.org
Founded in 1983, Family Research Council (FRC) is a nonprofit research and educational organization dedicated to articulating and advancing a family-centered philosophy of public life. In addition to providing policy research and analysis for the legislative, executive, and judicial branches of the federal government, FRC seeks to inform the news media, academic community, business leaders, and the general public about family issues that affect the nation. FRC's mission is to advance and defend faith, family, and freedom, in public policy and culture, from a Christian worldview. FRC's Watchmen on the Wall division is helping thousands of pastors and churches to have a stronger cultural impact in their own communities, cities, and states.

THE GLOBAL DAY OF PRAYER
http://www.globaldayofprayer.com
Each year, on Pentecost Sunday, millions of Christians from 220 nations unite in prayer. The event begins with 10 Days of Prayer followed by 90 Days of Blessing. Having "laid the foundation to saturate nations in prayer," organizers hope to "facilitate a lifestyle of prayer" among smaller groups of people worldwide.[2]

HARVEST PRAYER MINISTRIES
http://www.harvestprayer.com
Harvest Prayer Ministries (HPM), established in 1993, encourages local churches to pray for revival and world evangelization. HPM believes that God's purposes and plans for His church can only be established on a foundation of prayer. The ministry's core mission is to "transform lives by teaching prayer" and to "equip the local church to become a House of Prayer for all nations."[3]

INTERCESSORS FOR AMERICA

http://www.ifapray.org

Founded in 1973, Intercessors for America seeks God's intervention in governmental and cultural issues through fasting and prayer. The ministry not only keeps believers informed about current issues, but also encourages and equips them to intercede for America.

THE NATIONAL DAY OF PRAYER

http://www.nationaldayofprayer.org

The National Day of Prayer is an annual observance held on the first Thursday of May, inviting people of all faiths to pray for the nation. It was created in 1952 by a joint resolution of the United States Congress and signed into law by President Harry S. Truman. More than 40 thousand Christian events are organized annually across the country by the National Day of Prayer Task Force, led by Mrs. Shirley Dobson.

NATIONAL PASTORS' PRAYER NETWORK

http://www.nppn.org

The National Pastors' Prayer Network (NPPN) connects believers to God through prayer. The network also gathers pastors and prayer leaders together to pray for one another, their congregations, and communities across America and the world as they labor together to fulfill the Great Commission.

NATIONAL PRAYER COMMITTEE

https://nationalprayercommittee.com

The National Prayer Committee (NPC) fosters a number of projects, including the National Day of Prayer and *Prayer Connect* magazine.

204 PRAYER WARRIOR'S GUIDE TO SPIRITUAL BATTLE

PRAYER CONNECT MAGAZINE

http://www.prayerconnect.net

Prayer Connect is published by Harvest Prayer Ministries. The magazine keeps believers informed about what God is doing in the Prayer Movement, challenges them to grow in their prayer lives, and offers practical help and encouragement to increase their passion for prayer. No individual with a heart for intercession should be without *Prayer Connect.*

THE PRESIDENTIAL PRAYER TEAM

http://www.presidentialprayerteam.com

The independent, nonprofit organization behind the Presidential Prayer Team has a singular purpose: to encourage specific nationwide prayer for the president of the United States, as well as America, national leaders, and members of the military. The goal is to enlist at least 2.8 million participants, or one percent of the American population, to make this prayer commitment.

RECOMMENDED RESOURCES

Now it is time to put your training into action on the front lines. Get equipped and pray for our government, for the military, families, educators, businesses, the media and churches—each of the key centers of influence that impact our culture daily.

The National Day of Prayer Task Force offers a number of resources to equip prayer intercessors—all available online at www.NationalDayofPrayer.com. A few of the available prayer guides include:

A Time for Prayer will lead the reader through a better understanding of the importance of prayer, why we pray, timing of prayer, and prayers that support, guide, and strengthen. The book also includes a 30-day prayer guide, prayers from spiritual leaders, prayer tips, quotes, and selected Scriptures, all in a full-color, high-impact gift book. This book was designed to coincide with the National Day of Prayer and to be used as a source of renewal of your faith in the power of prayer.

For Such a Time as This: A 30-Day Prayer Guide for Our Nation is a handy, pocket-sized prayer guide for everyday use. The 30 days of prayer are focused on each of the seven centers of influence; this book is ideal for churches to distribute to their congregations to encourage and support the importance of daily prayer.

Heal Our Land is a 52-week prayer guide. Filled with biblical insight, prayer points, and daily direction, this complete prayer guide is the ideal resource for focused intercessory prayer. Join with thousands of pastors and churches in the growing prayer movement as we ask God for revival and transformation in our cities and nation.

Certain Peace in Uncertain Times tackles common questions: Is the world spinning out of control—and taking you with it? Do you long to replace constant worry with a sense of lasting tranquility? Join award-winning author Shirley Dobson to see how the remarkable gift of prayer has brought peace to her life and how it can do the same for you. Discover more about P.R.A.Y.—Praise, Repent, Ask, and Yield—a four-step approach to prayer that will lead you into a fulfilling, intimate relationship with God, the only true source of hope and security. This resource includes a 31-day prayer guide.

FURTHER RESOURCES

Blackaby, Henry, and Norman Blackaby. *Experiencing Prayer with Jesus: The Power of His Presence and Example*. Sisters, OR: Multnomah, 2006.

Bounds, E. M. *E. M. Bounds on Prayer*. New Kensington, PA: Whitaker House, 1997.

————. *The Weapon of Prayer*. New Kensington, PA: Whitaker House, 1996.

Christenson, Evelyn. *Praying God's Way*. Eugene, OR: Harvest House, 2003.

Crawford, Dan R., comp. *Giving Ourselves to Prayer: An Acts 6:4 Primer for Ministry*. Terre Haute, IN: Prayer Shop Publishing, 2009.

Dean, Jennifer Kennedy. *Heart's Cry: Principles of Prayer*. Birmingham: New Hope Publishers, 2007.

DeStefano, Anthony. *Ten Prayers God Always Says Yes To: Divine Answers to Life's Most Difficult Problems*. New York: Doubleday, 2007.

Fenner, Chris, comp. *Prayers of the Bible for Today*. Katy, TX: His Victory Publishing, 2009.

Hartley, Fred, III. *Prayer on Fire: What Happens When the Holy Spirit Ignites Your Prayers*. Colorado Springs: NavPress, 2006.

Helms, Elaine. *Prayer 101: What Every Intercessor Needs to Know*. Birmingham: New Hope Publishers, 2008.

Jeremiah, David. *The Prayer Matrix: Plugging into the Unseen Reality*. Sisters, OR: Multnomah, 2004.

Sproul, R. C. *The Prayer of the Lord*. Lake Mary, FL: Reformation Trust Publishing, 2009.

NOTES

2001 National Prayer

1. Psalm 33:12.

2. National Prayers are written yearly for the National Day of Prayer often by that year's Honorary Chairman. To learn more about the people who have filled this role, visit http://www.nationaldayofprayer.org/honorary_chairpersons.

Chapter 1: Call to War

1. Gary T. Meadors, "The Bible and Prayer," in *Giving Ourselves to Prayer: An Acts 6:4 Primer for Ministry*, comp. Dan R. Crawford (Terre Haute, IN: Prayer Shop Publishing), 10.

2. Adaptation of list compiled by AllAboutGOD.com, cited in "Why Pray?" National Day of Prayer Task Force, http://www.nationaldayofprayer.org (accessed October 6, 2010).

3. John Chrysostom, quoted in R. Kent Hughes, *James: Faith That Works* (Wheaton, IL: Crossway Books, 1991), 263.

4. The *Parade* Spirituality Poll, conducted by Insight Express, May 8–12, 2008, cited in Christine Wicker, "How Spiritual Are We?" October 4, 2009, http://www.parade.com/news/2009/10/04-how-spiritual-are-we.html (accessed October 6, 2010).

5. Federal Bureau of Investigation, Uniform Crime Reports, *Crime in the United States*, cited in Bureau of Justice Statistics, "Summary Findings," http://bjs.ojp.usdoj.gov/index.cfm?ty=tp&tid=3 (accessed October 6, 2010).

6. Jennifer Harper, "Study: Americans Pray Just to Get Through the Day," *Washington Times*, December 5, 2008, http://www.washingtontimes.com/news/2008/dec/05/study-americans-pray-just-to-get-through-the-day/.

7. National Day of Prayer Task Force, 2009 Media Kit, "Answer to Prayer," May 7, 2009.

8. Lawrence Jones, "Thousands Pray for Spiritual Revival at TheCall California," *Christian Post*, November 3, 2008, http://www.christianpost. com/article/20081103/thousands-pray-for-spiritual-revival-at-thecall-california/ (accessed October 7, 2010).

9. Adrienne S. Gaines, "National Day of Prayer May Be Largest-Ever," *Charisma* News Online, May 5, 2010, http://www.charismamag. com/~charisma/site-archives/570-news/featured-news/10838-national-day-of-prayer-may-be-largest-ever (accessed December 22, 2015).

10. National Day of Prayer Task Force, "National Day of Prayer 2015 Impact Report," November 16, 2015, http://www.nationaldayofprayer.org/impact_ report_post (accessed December 23, 2015).

11. Lifeway Research survey conducted April, May 2007, cited in Cathy Lynn Grossman, "Young Adults Aren't Sticking with Church," *USA Today*, August 6, 2007, http://usatoday30.usatoday.com/news/religion/2007-08-06-church-dropouts_N.htm (accessed December 23, 2015).

12. Frank D. Fincham, et al., "Spiritual Behaviors and Relationship Satisfaction: A Critical Analysis of the Role of Prayer," *Journal of Social and Clinical Psychology* 27, no. 4 (2008): 362–88.

13. M. G. Dudley and F. A. Kosinski, "Religiosity and Marital Satisfaction: A Research Note," *Review of Religious Research* 32 (1990): 78–86, cited in Fincham et al., "Spiritual Behaviors."

Chapter 2: The Baseline

1. Anthony DeStefano, *Ten Prayers God Always Says Yes To* (New York: Doubleday, 2007), 10–11.

2. R. C. Sproul, *The Holiness of God* (Wheaton, IL: Tyndale, 1985), 72.

3. Thomas Aquinas, "Man to the Image of God," cited in Millard J. Erickson, ed., *Readings in Christian Theology*, vol. 2, *Man's Need and God's Gift* (Grand Rapids: Baker Publishing Group, 1976), 37–43; Grace Communion International, "Humans in the Image of God," http://www.gci.org/humans/image (accessed October 7, 2010).

4. Leonard Verduin, "A Dominion-Haver," cited in Erickson, *Readings in Christian Theology*, 55–74; Grace Communion, "Humans in the Image of God."

5. G. W. Bromiley, "Image of God," cited in G. W. Bromiley, ed., *International Standard Bible Encyclopedia*, vol. 2 (Grand Rapids: Eerdmans, 1988), 804; Grace Communion, "Humans in the Image of God."

6. Emil Brunner, "Man and Creation," cited in Erickson, *Readings in Christian Theology*, 45–54; Grace Communion, "Humans in the Image of God."

2003 National Prayer

1. Proverbs 14:34.

Chapter 3: Enlisting: Understanding Prayer

1. Kenneth Brecher, "Galaxy," World Book Online Reference Center (2005), cited in World Book at NASA, s.v. "Galaxy," NASA, http://www.nasa.gov/worldbook/galaxy_worldbook.html (accessed October 9, 2010).

2. Jennifer Kennedy Dean, *Heart's Cry: Principles of Prayer* (Birmingham: New Hope Publishers, 2007), 18.

3. Fred A. Hartley, III, *Prayer on Fire: What Happens When the Holy Spirit Ignites Your Prayers* (Colorado Springs: NavPress, 2006), 16.

4. List compiled by All About God Ministries, http://www.AllAboutGod.com, cited on National Day of Prayer Task Force web site, http://www.nationaldayofprayer.org/what_is_prayer (accessed December 23, 2015).

5. Anthony DeStefano, *Ten Prayers God Always Says Yes To: Divine Answers to Life's Most Difficult Problems* (New York: Doubleday, 2007), 13.

6. Henry Blackaby and Norman Blackaby, *Experiencing Prayer with Jesus: The Power of His Presence and Example* (Sisters, OR: Multnomah), 28.

7. National Day of Prayer Task Force, "P.R.A.Y." (1994). Used by permission.

8. Shirley Dobson, *Certain Peace in Uncertain Times: Embracing Prayer in an Anxious Age* (Carol Stream, IL: Tyndale, 2008).

9. E. M. Bounds, *E. M. Bounds on Prayer* (New Kensington, PA: Whitaker House, 1997), 11, 19, 34–36, 42.

Chapter 4: Basic Training: The Fullness of Prayer

1. "Theory of Relativity: A Brief History," All About Science, http://www.allaboutscience.org/theory-of-relativity.htm (accessed October 10, 2010).

2. Wikipedia, s.v. "Special Relativity," http://en.wikipedia.org/wiki/Special_relativity; http://en.wikipedia.org/wiki/Principle_of_relativity (accessed October 10, 2010).

3. Wikipedia, s.v. "Large Hadron Collider," http://en.wikipedia.org/wiki/Large_Hadron_Collider (accessed October 10, 2010).

4. Craig Karges, *Ignite Your Intuition* (Deerfield Beach, FL: Health Communications, 1999), 15.

5. E. M. Bounds, *Purpose in Prayer* (New York: Fleming H. Revell Company, 1920), 47–48.

6. Robert Murray McCheyne, *The Purpose of Prayer* (Bellingham, WA: Logos Research Systems, 2004), 28.

Chapter 5: Advanced Training: Sustaining a Relationship

1. William Wilberforce, quoted in Becky Tirabassi, *Let God Talk to You* (Bloomington, MN: Bethany House Publishers, 2009), 105–06.

2. E. M. Bounds, *The Purpose of Prayer* (Bellingham, WA: Logos Research Systems, 2004), 16.

Chapter 7: The Home Front: Prayer and the Family

1. Rick Osborne, *Teaching your Child How to Pray* (Chicago: Moody Press, 1997), 34-43.

2. Barna Research Group, Ltd., "Protestants, Catholics and Mormons Reflect Diverse Levels of Religious Activity, July 9, 2001, https://www.barna.org/component/content/article/5-barna-update/45-barna-update-sp-657/54-protestants-catholics-and-mormons-reflect-diverse-levels-of-religious-activity#.Vnsmz5MrKRs (accessed December 23, 2015).

3. Barna Research Group, Ltd., "Americans Describe Sources of Spiritual Fulfillment and Frustration," November 29, 2004, https://www.barna.org/component/content/article/5-barna-update/45-barna-update-sp-657/199-americans-describe-sources-of-spiritual-fulfillment-and-frustration#.VnsmcpMrKRs (accessed December 23, 2015).

4. John Holmstrom, *When Prayers Are Answered* (New York: Penguin Group, 1995), 17–24.

5. *Miracles Are Heaven Sent* (Tulsa, OK: Honor Books, 1995), 93–94.

6. Linda Rutzen (National Day of Prayer staff), personal interview.

7. Kim Atamian, "Physicians Discovering That Prayer Can Be Potent Medicine," *Knight-Ridder/Tribute News Service*, July 10, 1996.

8. Debra Celovsky (National Day of Prayer volunteer coordinator) as told by Linda Rutzen (National Day of Prayer staff).

Chapter 8: Boot Camp: Mobilizing the Church

1. *Our Daily Bread*, April 24, 1983, quoted in Jared Brock, *A Year of Living Prayerfully* (Carol Stream, IL: Tyndale House Publishers, Inc., 2015), 303–04.

2009 National Prayer

1. Psalm 33:22.

Chapter 9: Strategic Planning: Approaching Prayer Intentionally

1. Headquarters, Department of the Army, *Field Manual No. 3-09.12 (6-121)*, June 2002, https://archive.org/stream/ost-military-doctrine-fm3_09x12/fm3_09x12_djvu.txt (accessed March 17, 2016).

2. Quoted in Jason Mandryk, *Pray for the World: A New Prayer Resource from Operation World* (Downers Grove, IL: InterVarsity Press, 2015), 73.

2010 National Prayer

1. Proclamation No. 97 (Mar. 30, 1863).

Chapter 10: Preparing for Battle

1. "14,000 Billion People Died in 14,000 Wars on Earth," *Pravda.ru*, June 10, 2009, http://english.pravda.ru/science/mysteries/06-10-2009/109689-criminal-0 (accessed December 23, 2015).
2. C. S. Lewis, *Mere Christianity* (New York: HarperOne, 2001), 135.
3. Francis Chan, *Crazy Love* (Colorado Springs: David C. Cook, 2008), 80.
4. Adrian Rogers, *The Full Armor of God*, tape, accessed August 18, 2008.

2012 National Prayer

1. Daniel 9:5 NKJV.

Chapter 12: The Weapons of Our Warfare

1. S. D. Gordon, *Quiet Talks in Prayer*, Christian Classics Ethereal Library (Chicago: Fleming H. Revell Company, 1904), n.p.
2. John Piper, *Let the Nations be Glad!* (Grand Rapids: Baker Academic, 2003), 45.
3. Charles Spurgeon, "The Shield of Faith" (sermon, Metropolitan Tabernacle, London, UK, October 27, 1861).
4. Greg Laurie, *The Great Compromise* (Word Publishing 1994), 62–63.
5. Beth Moore, *Praying God's Word* (Nashville: B&H Publishing Group, 2009), 5.

2013 National Prayer

1. Proclamation No. 97 (Mar. 30, 1863).

2014 National Prayer

1. Daniel 9:4–11 (author's paraphrase).

2015 National Prayer

1. John 8:32.

Chapter 15: The Warrior: Answer the Call

1. David Barton, *America: To Pray or Not to Pray?* (Aledo, TX: Wallbuilder Press, 1994), 58, 88. Used with permission.
2. From the records of the American Presidency Project, http://www.presidency.ucsb.edu/ws/index.php (accessed December 23, 2015).
3. E. M. Bounds, *The Weapon of Prayer* (Grand Rapids, MI: Christian Classics Ethereal Library, 2004), 26.
4. "The Lausanne Covenant," The Lausanne Movement (1974), www.lausanne.org/covenant; "The Manila Manifesto," The Lausanne Movement (1989), www.lausanne.org/all-documents/manila-manifesto.html (accessed October 12, 2010).
5. E. M. Bounds, *The Weapon of Prayer*, 30–31.

6. Williams Direct, "Churches and Clergy," www.churchladies.com/break-down.pdf (accessed December 23, 2015).

7. Sally C. Curtin, Joyce C. Abma, Stephanie J. Ventura, and Stanley K. Henshaw, "Pregnancy rates for U.S. women continue to drop," Centers for Disease Control and Prevention, December 2013, http://www.cdc.gov/nchs/data/databriefs/db136.htm (accessed March 21, 2016).

8. Author unknown.

Special Section: A Field Guide for Family Prayer

1. "How to Lead Your Child to Christ," used by permission, Chariot Victor Publishing.

2. Some of the ideas in this section are adapted from the books *Faithful Parents, Faithful Kids* by Greg P. Johnson and Mike Yorkey (Tyndale) and *Raising Responsible Kids* by Jay Kesler.

3. John W. Cowart, *Why Don't I Get What I Pray For?* (Downers Grove, IL: InterVarsity Press, 1993), 7.

4. Henry Blackaby, *Experiencing God: Knowing and Doing His Will* (Nashville, Tennessee: Broadman and Holman Publishers, 1993).

5. James C. Dobson, *When God Doesn't Make Sense* (Wheaton, Illinois: Tyndale House Publishers, 1993), 68–69.

Recommended Ministries

1. "About Us," Christian Legal Society, http://www.clsnet.org/page.aspx?pid=820 (accessed January 19, 2016).

2. "History," Global Day of Prayer, http://www.globaldayofprayer.com/index.php/about-us/history/ (accessed January 19, 2016).

3. "Home," Harvest Prayer Ministries, http://www.harvestprayer.com/ (accessed January 19, 2016).

★ ★ ★

ABOUT THE AUTHORS

JOHN BORNSCHEIN

John Bornschein is the senior pastor of Calvary Fellowship Fountain Valley. He is also the vice chairman of the National Day of Prayer Task Force and an executive member of the National Prayer Committee. His 19 years in ministry span a range of vast responsibilities, including time as a missionary and senior pastor and service with Mission of Mercy (later One Child Matters), Heritage Builders, Focus on the Family, and the National Day of Prayer Task Force.

John is the Executive Producer of *Drive Thru History: America,* the latest video curriculum in the popular series seen on History Channel International and Trinity Broadcasting Network. As an executive producer, John has also worked alongside some of the best creative minds in Nashville to create powerful patriotic and worship music, including "Let Freedom Ring" by Dennis Jernigan (Doxology Records), "America" with Rebecca St. James (ForeFront Records), and "We Pray" with BarlowGirl (Fervent).

As an author, John has contributed to dozens of resources, including the books *Heal Our Land, Compassion Revolution, Start Your Family, Together in Prayer,* and *Celebration Parenthood* as well as *A Prayer Warrior's Guide to Spiritual Battle* and *For Life* (both with Kirkdale Press). In addition, he has written for publications including *Horizon*, *Prayer Lines* and *Focus on the Family*.

John is a frequent guest on television and radio programs across the nation (including TBN, Fox News, TheBlaze TV, GOD TV, Daystar Television, and *Family Talk* with Dr. James Dobson) and has hosted the Focus on the Family broadcast and *Life Today* on Salem networks. He is the host of the *Engage in Truth* radio show heard on 100.7 KGFT and a speaker at the popular *Spiritual Growth of Children* conferences attended by thousands around the country.

John has studied business and theology and is currently pursuing a Master of Divinity degree from Bethany Baptist Seminary. He also teaches at the CFFV Academy, an extension of the Ligonier Academy led by R. C. Sproul. John has served at the United Nations in New York and with congressional leaders in Washington, D.C., as a representative for the National Day of Prayer. But his true joy is his wife, Brandi, and their five children, who love the Lord. They reside in Colorado Springs, Colorado.

DAVID BUTTS

David received a bachelor of arts degree from Lincoln Christian College in 1975 and bachelor's (1978) and master's (1982) degrees from Indiana State University. In 2014 he received a Doctor of Philosophy in Theology (PhD) from Atlantic Coast Theological Seminary. He served as associate minister at several Terre Haute churches before moving to Kansas, Illinois, in 1982 to become senior minister of Kansas Christian Church. It was in Kansas that David's passion for prayer and missions began to develop. He has served, and continues to serve, in numerous leadership capacities and on boards of directors and committees, including America's National Prayer Committee as chairman, the Denominational Prayer Leaders Network as secretary and treasurer, Pioneer Bible Translators as chairman of the board of directors, and Mission America Coalition as a member of the executive committee.

David has authored articles on prayer and missions for several magazines, including *Christian Standard*, *The Lookout*, *Horizons*, and *Pray!* He is the author of *The Devil Goes to Church*, *Pray Like the King* (with his wife, Kim), and *Asleep in the Land of Nod*. He has also completed a videotape presentation on "Leadership for a Praying Church."

KATHY BRANZELL

Kathy is the founder, president, and CEO of Fellowship and Christian Encouragement (FACE) for Educators, which is an interdenominational Christian ministry serving public, private, and home educators. FACE is one of the fastest growing Christian ministries in the United States, with prayer chapters motivating and encouraging educators throughout the United States and around the world. Kathy also manages an independent educational consulting and speaking practice. She is a member of America's National Prayer Committee and a founding member of the Mission America Public School Ministries Coalition and IAM4schools.com, where she worked on special projects with Secretary of Education Rod Paige and President George W. Bush's Office of Faith-Based and Community Initiatives.

Kathy also partners with the Luis Palau Evangelistic Association and travels throughout the United States to assist in hosting the Great Music! Good News! Festival's educator brunch. Her focus is on the encouragement and improvement of teachers, children, educational leadership, and those who support the educational process. Kathy can also be heard daily on New Life Radio stations, giving encouragement during her one-minute "Lesson Plan for Life" devotionals.

Prior to assuming her present positions, Kathy served on North Carolina Governor Jim Hunt's educational commission, Smart Start. Kathy was a grant-management consultant and was responsible for evaluating childcare facilities, technical assistance, and educator training. Her efforts contributed to millions of dollars in federal and state funding to central North Carolina education programs. During this period, she also served as an adjunct professor at Fayetteville Technical Community College and conducted motivational and subject matter workshops at numerous colleges, churches, schools, and professional conferences. In 1995 and 1996, she served as an instructor for the Early Childhood Development Program at the University of Georgia, Athens, and from 1992 to 1994 she worked as Regional Trainer and Curriculum Developer at KinderCare in Chicago, Illinois. From 1988 to 1992, she held numerous educational positions, including Head Start instructor, special needs instructor, and kindergarten teacher.

Kathy attended the University of Georgia, Athens, where she received a bachelor of education degree in 1990, with a specialization in early childhood education and child development. She is married to her childhood sweetheart, Russell, and is the proud mother of two children, Chandler and Emily Sara.

DION ELMORE

Dion has served as Director of the National Day of Prayer Task Force. He is passionate about expository teaching of God's Word and effectively equipping and mobilizing the church for prayer and service. The Scripture that keeps the church focused is Acts 2:42: "And [the believers] continued steadfastly in the apostles' doctrine and fellowship, in the breaking of bread, and in prayers" (NKJV).

Dion is a visionary leader and an advocate of developing unique, self-sustaining ministry outreaches through the local church into the local community. These outreaches and organizations connect with individuals and families who may not otherwise come into a local church.

Prior to entering full-time pastoral ministry, Dion was a leader in both corporate and small-business environments, specializing in development, marketing, and advertising. He also served for several years with Focus on the Family and was a leader in the development and marketing of films, books, magazines, and radio dramas, including the Adventures in Odyssey series. He also was involved in Focus on the Family's international efforts, working to establish ministry outreaches in the United Kingdom, Australia, New Zealand, and South Africa.

Dion lives in Colorado Springs, Colorado with his wife, Ann, and their children, Sarah, Rachel, Hannah, and Caleb.

BRIAN R. TOON

Brian is a retired navy captain with 25 years of leadership experience. He has a proven track record leading large organizations, including a nuclear-warfare command center, aircraft carrier air and flight-deck operations, and a naval aviation squadron. He has a master of business administration (MBA) from the University of Nebraska, Lincoln, a master's degree in National Security and Strategic Policy from the Naval War College in Newport, Rhode Island, and a bachelor's degree in Business Administration from the University of Colorado Boulder. An excellent communicator, Brian has participated in numerous interviews on national television networks, including CNN, MSNBC, and ABC, and has been interviewed by the Los Angeles Times and Detroit Free Press. He has also been featured on the British Broadcasting Corporation network (BBC) while serving as Air Boss on the aircraft carrier Abraham Lincoln during Operation Iraqi Freedom. Brian is married and has four children and two grandchildren.

JOIN THE PRAYER MOVEMENT ONLINE

Tweet your favorite quote from *A Prayer Warrior's Guide to Spiritual Battle*—#PrayerWarrior.

Share your thoughts—write a review of this book on Vyrso.com, Amazon.com, Goodreads.com, or your blog.

Visit NationalDayofPrayer.org, follow @NationalPrayer on Twitter, or connect with the National Day of Prayer Task Force on Facebook for the latest on the Prayer Movement.

Check out KirkdalePress.com or follow @KirkdalePress for more books from John Bornschein and other prayer leaders.

And most importantly: Pray!